TWAYNE'S WORLD AUTHORS SERIES
A Survey of the World's Literature

SPAIN

Janet W. Díaz, University of North Carolina, Chapel Hill
Gerald E. Wade, Vanderbilt University

EDITORS

Bartolomé de Torres Naharro

TWAS 522

Scenes from the *Comedia Aquilana* of Bartolomé de Torres Naharro

BARTOLOMÉ
DE TORRES NAHARRO

By JOHN LIHANI

University of Kentucky

TWAYNE PUBLISHERS

A DIVISION OF G. K. HALL & CO., BOSTON

Copyright © 1979 by G. K. Hall & Co.

Published in 1979 by Twayne Publishers,
A Division of G. K. Hall & Co.
All Rights Reserved

Printed on permanent/durable acid-free paper and bound
in the United States of America

First Printing

Library of Congress Cataloging in Publication Data

Lihani, John.
Bartolomé de Torres Naharro.

(Twayne's world authors series ; TWAS 522 : Spain)
Bibliography: p. 171–74
Includes index.
1. Torres Naharro, Bartolomé de, fl. 1517—Criticism
and interpretation.
PQ6437.T76Z78   1979   862'.3   78-11221
ISBN 0-8057-6363-5

To my parents

About the Author

John Lihani is Professor of Medieval and Renaissance Spanish Literature and Hispanic Linguistics at the University of Kentucky. After graduating from Western Reserve University, (B.S., *magna cum laude*) in 1948, he went to The Ohio State University for the M.A. degree. After obtaining the Ph.D. in Romance Languages from the University of Texas in 1954, his teaching of literature and linguistics has taken him to the faculties of Tulane University, the University of Texas, Yale University, University of Pittsburgh, and the Instituto Caro y Cuervo.

Recipient of various fellowships and awards, including the Morse Fellowship from Yale University, a grant from the Spanish government for postdoctoral studies at the University of Madrid, a Fulbright professorship in linguistics to Colombia, S.A. (1965–66), and awards from the International Research and Exchanges Board, and the American Philosophical Society have enabled him to teach, study and do research in many parts of North America, South America, Eastern and Western Europe. Born in Czechoslovakia (he is Slovak by birth, American by choice, Spanish by profession, and all three by affection), John Lihani possesses a working knowledge of over a dozen languages. He has authored forty professional articles, several books, including an edition of Lucas Fernández, *Farsas y églogas* (1969), a major study of *El lenguaje de Lucas Fernández; estudio del dialecto sayagués* (1973), a Twayne monograph on *Lucas Fernández,* and other works. Professor Lihani has served as chairman and organizer for national and regional groups of professional organizations, and has served in university advisory posts and diverse professional committees. He holds membership in the Modern Language Association of America, the American Association of Teachers of Spanish and Portuguese, and has rendered editorial duties as the founding Editor of *La corónica*, Associate Editor of *Bulletin of the 'Comediantes,'* member of the Editorial Board of the *Kentucky Romance Quarterly,* and as referee reader for critical periodicals and university presses.

Preface

Bartolomé de Torres Naharro is an outstanding Spanish playwright of the sixteenth century. Most of his work was composed and performed in Italy where it was first compiled and published under the title of *Propalladia* (1517). In the following chapters we attempt to present his life and to evaluate his works through the analytical and critical study of the material available. Torres Naharro learned his trade both from the classical and humanistic Latin drama, and the contemporary Italian and Spanish theaters. After his participation in the Salamancan school of dramatists, he embarked on new directions setting a pace for the stage far ahead of his time—a pace that was equaled only with the onset of the greatest Spanish playwrights of the baroque period.

His importance in the continuum of the Iberian and European theater is exemplified in the presentation of his dramaturgic credo, in the *Prohemio*, which appears as a preface to his works. This brief but important document marks him as the first dramatic critic in Spain. The precepts therein served as a guide to him and to generations of playwrights that followed. Torres Naharro first presents the views on comedy and tragedy held by the ancients, then Tullio's interpretation of comedy and Acron's classification of six types of comedy with its four parts; next he notes Horace's stipulation of five acts for a play and stresses his adherence to decorum. Then the author launches into his own views, which we translate as follows:[1]

And I say this: that comedy is nothing more than an ingenious production of notable and finally happy incidents, explained by people. Its division into five acts not only seems good to me, but very necessary; although I call them journeys (*jornadas*), because they seem more like resting places than anything else.[2] As a result, the comedy is better understood and performed. Regarding the number of people who are to be involved, it is my preference that they should not be so few that it might appear a mute festival, nor so many that they might cause confusion. Although in our *Comedia Tinellaria* [*Mess Hall Comedy*] there were more than twenty individuals, because its topic did not permit fewer, the proper number it seems to me ought to be from six up to twelve persons. The decorum in the comedies is like the rudder of a ship, which the good playwright should always keep before him. Decorum is a precise and proper combination of the material, that is to say: assigning to each his own, avoiding improper things, making use of all legitimate ones, so that the slave will not say, nor do deeds that are only behooving of a master, and vice versa; and [it means] saddening a sad place and enlivening a joyful place, with all the care, diligence, and means possible, etc.

As to the origins of drama and why it is called comedy, there are so many opinions that they are simply confusing. As regards the types of comedies, it seems to me that two should suffice for our Castilian language: *comedia a noticia* ["documentary comedy"] and *comedia a fantasía* ["fictional comedy"]. By *a noticia* ["documentary"] is meant that it is about events witnessed and seen in reality and in truth, as are the *Soldadesca* ["military"] and *Tinellaria* ["mess hall"] comedies; *a fantasía* ["fictional"] that it is about imagined or feigned events that have the coloring of, though it is not, truth, as are the *Seraphina*, *Ymenea*, etc. Regarding parts of comedy, again two should suffice, namely: introit and argument ["story"]. Should anyone think that there ought to be more of one or of the other, the wise readers have permission to add or remove as they please. Likewise, they will find in parts of my work some Italian words, especially in the comedies, which were advisable to use, taking into consideration the place where, and the people for whom, they were performed. Some of them I have removed, others I have left in, since they are not meant to undermine our Castilian language, but rather to enrich it.[3]

Thus, Torres Naharro, as one of the early significant practitioners and theoreticians of histrionic art, codifies and promulgates his formula of artistic principles in Spanish. Those who may wish to pursue the topic further can find the original in any of the editions of Torres Naharro's complete works as listed in the bibliography. For a basis of our discussions we present a detailed summary of each story, advisable since the plays are written at times in several languages and following their plots may be a difficult task. The comprehensive summaries help the reader through his own empirical experience to determine for himself the techniques used and the standards formulated by the playwright for his success in the theater.

Literature is often considered a form of history—history on an individual or personalized level. Balzac felt that the novel set down an individualized history of nations. Because of its depiction of individuals in their life patterns, literature can indeed be equated with personalized history. A great portion of the value of Torres

Preface

Naharro's works lies in this very nature of history. He clearly presents people in their environments. It is impossible in one book to discuss all the features of the playwright's art and to cover the human aspects of that period found in his writings. Therefore, we have varied our approach to each play as suggested by its structure and contents. Sometimes our chapters emphasize structural entities, other times thematic diversities. The same type of critical judgment that appears segmented in the different chapters can often be applied in a similar manner to the other plays for evaluative purposes. We attempt to consolidate previous research, incorporate new thoughts, and supply a fresh approach to the author's production. These procedures afford opportunities to reinforce and approve, or conversely to question and challenge some of our statements and observations. The persistent presence of drama is as durable and involved as that of human civilization. Torres Naharro is recognized as one of the most remarkable figures in the history of modern European drama, and his works constitute a significant segment in the theater's long and fascinating history.

JOHN LIHANI

University of Kentucky

Acknowledgments

The credits are so many and the assistance I received from others has covered such a long period of time, that I have often had occasion to express them and personally to recognize gratefully my many benefactors. It is a rewarding task once again for me to be able to assign credit to all those who have contributed in some measure to the formation of this book. I am indebted to my many mentors for sharing their views with me, as well as my students, whom I consider rather as my friends, who have challenged, worked out, or otherwise shared some of their ideas on the theater with mine. Among these I would like to single out Dr. E. M. Malinak whose interest in Torres Naharro prompted long and friendly discussions that generated many exchanges of fruitful ideas.

I am grateful to my colleagues of the University of Kentucky, Dr. Louis Swift of the Department of Classics, whose advice has been most enlightening, and Dr. W. F. Prizer of the Department of Music, who helped in the search of certain archives in Italy. Furthermore, I am indebted to D. Florencio Marcos, archivist of the University of Salamanca, for the data which he so generously provided, and to many other colleagues who, like Dr. Charlotte Stern, contributed valuable information through correspondence, and also to the co-editors, Dr. Gerald E. Wade and Dr. Janet W. Díaz, for their exacting work. Finally, the personal research that was accomplished here and abroad would have been impossible without the financial support from the University of Kentucky Research Foundation and the American Philosophical Society. To all these and others whom I have not mentioned but to whom I am indebted, I reiterate my gratitude.

Chronology

1480– Suggested period for birth of Bartolomé de Torres Naharro in
1485 Torre de Miguel Sesmero (Western Spain), apparently of
      Moorish or Judaic origins.

1496 Possibly a part-time actor with Juan del Encina.

1496 Thought to be attending University of Salamanca, with
      opportunity to meet Lucas Fernández, Rodrigo Basurto, and
      Fernando de Rojas.

1498 Possibly shares job of cantor in Cathedral of Salamanca with
      Lucas Fernández.

1503 Arrives in Rome as a cleric or soldier, possibly working for
      Cesare Borgia (1476–1507); mingles with Spanish writers and
      Italian Humanists.

1505 Composes *Diálogo del nascimiento* and *Addición del diálogo*
      (alternate dates suggested, 1504–1512).

1508 Composes *Comedia Seraphina* (alternate dates, 1515–1517).

1509 Torres Naharro's *Comedia Jacinta* possibly figures in the
      nuptial celebrations of Vittoria Colonna and Fernando de
      Ávalos.

1510 *Comedia Soldadesca* composed.

1513 Possibly enters service of Giovanni de Medici (later Pope
      Leo X, 1513–1521) or Giulio de Medici (later Pope Clement
      VII, 1523–1534). During this period, writes many of his
      shorter poems.

1514 Probably in Rome, presenting a play honoring Isabella
      d'Este.

1514 Presents *Comedia Trophea* at the Vatican; possible repeat
      performance of *Comedia Jacinta*.

1516 Leaves Medicis, entering service of Cardinal de Sancta Cruz,
      Bernardino de Carvajal. Presentation of *Comedia Tinel-
      laria* and *Comedia Ymenea*.

1517 Leaves Rome, entering service of the Fabrizio Colonna fam-
      ily in Naples; employed by the son-in-law, Fernando de
      Ávalos, husband of Vittoria Colonna. *Propalladia* pub-
      lished in Naples.

1519 Probable composition of *Comedia Calamita*.

parochial school in his home town. Eventually, he may have gone on
to the University of Salamanca, as Marcelino Menéndez y Pelayo has
supposed, either as a servant (capigorrón) to a wealthy boy,[4] or
perhaps even as a student in his own right. Torres Naharro reminisces about school days in his works, though he provides no
satisfactory evidence for singling out any particular school. He
speaks in general terms of students studying by bright moonlight in
order to economize on candles (II, 470, 30–34), but gives a specific
clue only when he names a professor of physics and astrology at the
University of Salamanca, Rodrigo Basurto. Mention of Basurto's
name bespeaks the latter's fame and suggests Torres Naharro's acquaintance with the educator. Records at the University of
Salamanca as well as those of the University of Valladolid have been
thoroughly researched for Bartolomé de Torres Naharro, but nothing documents his possible training at either place. Matriculation
records begin only in 1546, long after Torres Naharro would have
been there; consequently the search has proved unfruitful.

As suggested in an above note: it appears that some of Encina's
verses can be interpreted to indicate a personal relationship between him and Torres Naharro. In view of the possible circumstances pertaining to Juan del Encina (1461–1529), and to Encina's cousin and professional competitor, Lucas Fernández, it
would appear that both Encina and Fernández personally knew
Torres Naharro at some time in their lives. In the documents that
refer to a contest of candidates for the position of cantor in the
Cathedral of Salamanca, there is mention of the three youths who
were finally asked to share the position, and one of them was a
Bartolomé (whose last name is not given, but who could conceivably
be the dramatist of our study). The tripartite division of the cantor's
job was determined in 1498, which, if one accepts Gillet's guess of
1485 as the birth year of Torres Naharro, would make Bartolomé
barely thirteen years old at the time.

When Juan del Encina was in need of actors for plays in the
household of the duke of Alba during the years 1492–1498 (when he
served as director of palatial entertainment), it is likely that he
would choose those youths available to him from the student body at
the local university with which he had close ties. Thus, such
talented youths as Bartolomé de Torres Naharro, Lucas Fernández,
Gil Vicente, and Diego Sánchez de Badajoz, among others, who
possessed inherent theatrical inclinations, would learn their his-

trionic trade as apprentices under the masterful tutelage and expert direction of Encina.[5]

As was typical of the educational system of the day, Torres Naharro obtained a thorough foundation in the classics; he may have concentrated his studies at Salamanca on preparation for the priesthood. Years later, he was indeed ordained as a priest in the very diocese in which he is believed to have been born. An inkling of this ordination comes in the form of a papal privilege for the publication of the *Propalladia* in 1517 in which Torres Naharro is referred to as a cleric of the diocese of Badajoz, *Clericus Pacensis diocesis* (I, 145; IV, 402).

Torres Naharro does not appear to have been content solely with administering to the spiritual needs of his community—at least not in his youth. His was a restless, dynamic personality, as suited to a life of soldiering as to one of religion. What may have been his native Extremadura was, after all, a region which provided much of the bellicose, conquering spirit for the conquests of the New World.[6] Although Torres Naharro showed little inclination for the New World, mentioning some of its products in one of his plays, he did seek adventure and a better livelihood away from his homeland, in the Italian territories conquered earlier by Spain. It is not surprising then that Bartolomé de Torres Naharro should have decided to relinquish, postpone, or to put aside the cleric's robes temporarily and to take up soldiering. There is no direct evidence on the military phase of Torres Naharro's life; several critics, including Joseph E. Gillet, have surmised that his knowledge of army life, vividly described in the *Comedia Soldadesca*, is such that he must have acquired it through personal experience (IV, 403). His allusions to Valencia and places in Andalusia, such as the city of Seville, presumably reflect his acquaintance with these places from his travels and from his duties as a soldier in the service of the Catholic kings. As a military man, Torres Naharro probably traveled throughout the Valencian and Catalonian provinces where he learned the speech of these particular regions, later utilized in such plays as the *Comedia Seraphina* and the *Comedia Tinellaria*.

As a soldier he evidently embarked from Valencia for Rome in 1502, and may have been captured by Islamic pirates, although it is uncertain whether they were Turkish, Arabic, or of mixed nationality (IV, 403). Textual evidence in his works suggests that he himself was a Christian convert from Islam.[7] His captivity was relatively brief, and it seems doubtful whether he was actually taken to Algiers, as was Cervantes later. Torres Naharro was ransomed and completed his original journey to Rome. His detention does not seem to have been particularly unique and for that reason not particularly memorable. Indeed, there is no reference to it in his writings, except for the mention of a corsair raid near Rome that may have involved him directly.[8] References to sea voyages and duties aboard ship reflect his exposure to the mariner's trade. Torres Naharro probably reached Rome between 1503 and 1507 and, when about eighteen, apparently served in the military outfits trained and maintained by Cesare Borgia at Faenza, Forli, Rimini; Torres Naharro may also have personally witnessed the battle of Chirinola in 1503.

The close contacts between Spain and Italy were highlighted by King Fernando's visit in 1506 to Naples. There are indications to substantiate that Spanish and Italian families kept close, amiable relationships for many generations. In 1507 a contract of marriage was signed between Fernando de Ávalos of Spanish origin and Vittoria Colonna of Roman ancestry, and they were married two years later on December 27, 1509, on the Isle of Ischia, when both were nineteen years old.[9] Torres Naharro, already in Italy, may have been one of the chief entertainers at the engagement or at the wedding's festivities of this couple, and perhaps followed Fernando de Ávalos to battle against the French in Ravenna in 1512, where Fernando was wounded. Shortly thereafter, while still in his early twenties, Torres Naharro established residence in Rome. In all likelihood perfecting his literary talents at this time, he probably produced his first full-length plays, the *Comedia Seraphina* and the *Comedia Soldadesca* (1508–1510), after trying his hand at the Christmas marriage play, *Diálogo del nascimiento* (1505–1507).

It is uncertain as to just when Bartolomé managed to obtain a benefactor and literary patron to subsidize him in a household full of other servants and entertainers that he presented in subsequent works. Nor is it known whether Torres Naharro joined a traveling troupe of players in Italy and thus served out his theatrical apprenticeship. He could have become affiliated with Spanish or even Italian actors in presenting plays like Encina's *Égloga de Plácida y Vitoriano*, performed in Rome in 1513 in the palace of the Spanish cardinal.[10] Whether officially a cleric or not, it is nonetheless supposed that as early as 1513 he found a position in the home of some noble, perhaps Giulio de Medici, in whose palace he served when Medici was a cardinal , or in the home of Giovanni de Medici who became Pope Leo X (1513–1523).[11] Giulio de Medici became Pope Clement VII in 1523. Before Torres Naharro became an entertainer in the cardinal's palace, he had proved his ability by writing his first plays, as well as many poems and ballads of earlier vintage.

He probably accompanied his early protector on ceremonial visits throughout Italy to nobles' palaces from Mantua to Naples and Ischia, presenting his own plays along with those of other writers for the delectation of the selected theatrical public that included Renaissance women like Isabella d'Este and Vittoria Colonna.[12] Noble marriages and public office swearing-in ceremonies provided occasions to display his dramatic talents, and like Encina, also in Italy at the time, he found fertile soil. This period of Italian residency was the time of his greatest creative activity and afforded Torres Naharro opportunities to see performances of Italian humanistic plays at weddings, public gatherings, banquets, and other festive occasions. Italy had several active playwrights during Torres Naharro's lifetime. Their plays as well as those of others who preceded them were being presented. Thus the Spanish writer had chances to become familiar with the works of Ariosto, Nardi, Machiavelli, Bibbiana, Aretino, Furlovisi, Piccolomini, Armonio, Zambarti, and Dalochne. These playwrights (who flourished between 1300 and 1550) continued the tradition of Plautus and Terence. Many of their plays are still in existence, and together with those by other Spaniards and Italians, they provided the groundwork on which Torres Naharro could develop his own talents.

In 1516 Torres Naharro had apparently changed his employer. He left the service of Giulio de Medici late in 1515 and entered the household of Cardinal Bernardino de Carvajal, a Spaniard like himself. He is probably referring to himself in the *Comedia Soldadesca* when he writes, "Luego quiero/ hablar con un compañero/ qu' es plático y andaluz,/ que está con vn camarero/ del Cardenal Sancta Cruz" ("Later I want to speak with a friend who's a soldier and Andalusian, who's with a chamberlain of Cardinal Sancta Cruz") (II, 153, 220–24). The Cardinal de Sancta Cruz was Bernardino de Carvajal.

But he encountered rivals for his job in Carvajal's palace. One of these, a laborious poet, was probably Alonso Hernández (IV, 409). There were other less personal but more professional rivals, writers

like Juan del Encina, Diego Ávila, Rodrigo de Reinosa, and Díaz
Tanco de Fregenal. Encina vied with Torres Naharro for the favor of
the Spanish colony as he too sought to make a living entertaining it.
Encina had indeed found great favor among the Spanish clergy and
populace upon his arrival in Rome. There was a circle of other
acquaintances around him whose names can be verified even to this
day. Gillet lists Francisquino, Hernando Merino, Barberius, and
Johannes Murconius (IV, 410) from among the ten thousand or so
Spaniards then living in Rome and accounting for one-sixth of the
city's total population. They had their own churches, their own
hospitals, book stores, restaurants, taverns, and schools. In their
midst Torres Naharro spent several years.

But Bartolomé de Torres Naharro's service with Cardinal Carvajal
lasted only about a year, when he unexpectedly left Rome. Fortunately he soon managed to place himself in the protection of Fabrizio Colonna in Naples. Fabrizio was well known as the protagonist
of Machiavelli's book on the art of war and as the former general of
Pope Julius II. Colonna's intercession in 1517 provided Torres
Naharro with a job in the service of Don Fernando de Ávalos,
marquis of Pescara and husband of Fabrizio's daughter, Vittoria
Colonna. By this time Torres Naharro had written a sufficient
number of plays to compile them in a work which he chose to entitle
Propalladia (*First Fruits of Pallas*—the goddess of wisdom). The collection which came off the press in Naples on March 26, 1517, was
dedicated with profound gratitude to Fabrizio Colonna. Bartolomé
continued writing, acting, and directing, but an inborn wanderlust,
cynicism, and dissatisfaction with life pushed him onward again; he
was not long in Naples. It is supposed that he returned to Spain, and
this time on a somewhat more permanent basis, to the city of
Seville. Here an augmented edition of his *Propalladia* was published in 1520 containing one new additional play, the *Comedia
Calamita*. A 1524 edition published in Naples added the final play,
the *Comedia Aquilana*, to the collection. Torres Naharro's growth in
popularity is attested to by the nine other editions of his works in
the sixteenth century along with several editions of single plays and
isolated poems (I, 5–127).

According to the available documents, as well as intuitive deduc-
tions, it seemed to Gillet that Torres Naharro may have died in
Seville about the year 1520 or 1524 (IV, 417). Since poems by the
author appeared during the decade of the 1520s, Menéndez y

Pelayo has suggested the possible year of his death to be 1530.[13] This is conjectural, and it is possible that he lived on in a more stable and less notorious vocation, perhaps in education or in the ministry, reaching a much more advanced age than has been previously thought. If for the moment we take 1480 or 1485 as the year of Torres Naharro's birth, then he was at most forty or fifty years old at the time of his death, if this occurred between 1520 and 1530.

There are two or three Bartolomé de Torre(s) in Spanish encyclopedias or archives, and on occasion the facts pertaining to their lives seem to mesh or become confused. As suggested in note 2, the most likely possibility for further investigation appears to have been Bartolomé de Torres, an eminent theologian, who served as bishop of the Canary Islands from 1566 to 1568. An attempt to determine whether he may have been a schismatic offshoot of our Bartolomé de Torres Naharro was undertaken. Despite noticeable similarities in name, character, and inclination, there remained the problem of year of birth. The theologian claimed to be about fifty years old in 1562, and if this claim is taken literally, it precludes identifying him as Torres Naharro because the latter was already in Italy composing plays at the time of this Torres' birth. Two other instances of identical names, Bartolomé de Torres, were checked out. One turned out to be a master of arts from the University of Alcalá (ca. 1516); another, a Dominican monk, figured prominently in the reforms of this religious order in Castile in the first years of the sixteenth century. Neither biography seems to coincide with what we know of the dramatist.[14] Another coincidence of the name appears in a later generation with an actor, but it is not known whether there might have been any relationship with our dramatist. Recently, Father Enrique Llamas of the order of Carmelitas Descalzos in Madrid has discovered a new work by the theologian, which he is preparing for publication. At this writing, regrettably the problems alluded to above remain unresolved.

In the absence of further documentary evidence, we must look for clues to this writer's existence in the compositions he has left us. The work of Torres Naharro adds to our knowledge of him as an individual personality. The thoughts and ideas that reflect this man are distributed in his poetry and drama of the *Propalladia*. Many spiritual aspects of the man will be brought out in the various studies comprising the chapters that follow.

of pessimism or fatalism and a vein of sadness surface repeatedly in his poems. He expects nothing good from life, and sinks into resignation before it. His pessimism is infected with sadness, evidenced by the use of the words *triste* ("sad") or *tristeza* ("sadness"): *tristeza me sobra* ("I have more than enough sadness") (I, 158, 4), *tristes agüeros* ("sad omens") (I, 155, 24), and *la triste carne mia* ("my sad flesh") (I, 155, 17). The sadness seems at times to penetrate his entire being.

Expectedly, various sides of his personality come to the fore in his poems. The poet is overwhelmed with frustration and futility, believing that he has no control over destiny. Predestination and fatalism are his guides: "ni puedo acertar en cosa que quiera" ("I can't succeed in whatever I want") (I, 156, 28); "poco vale diligencia/ contra el mal predistinado" ("diligence has little value against predestined evil") (I, 255, 35–36). He sees no remedy, "Con amistad y sin ella,/ siempre tengo mala vida" ("With or without friendship, I always have a bad life") (I, 169, 29–30), and suggests that he cannot control his life: "Ya que no por culpa mía/ pierdo amigos y amistad" ("Since not through my fault I lose friends and friendship") (I, 171, 78–79). Friendship seems to have been hard to cultivate for him and what there was of it was particularly endangered in the heartless city of Rome: "la dulce amistad/ por esta sancta ciudad/ veo andar tan peligrosa" ("the sweet friendship I see run such danger in this Holy City") (I, 169, 3–5). Torres Naharro was a fatalist, interposing symbolic figures such as Fate or Fortune between human creatures and God. Although the Spanish Inquisition was generally lenient in its treatment of the *Propalladia,* it did delete a fatalistic reference to predestination in the expurgated edition of his works in 1573.[1]

Being as vain as most other human beings, Torres Naharro considered himself righteous and did not like to be ridiculed: "burlar de los justos se llama deporte" ("to play practical jokes on good people is called a sport") (I, 156, 40). Repeatedly he confessed a strong desire to love; indeed, his devotion would seem to have been at times somewhat excessive. It espoused complete service and sentimental surrender, "pues que te fui obediente/ desd'el punto que te vi" ("since I was obedient to you from the moment I saw you") (I, 182, 37–38). He was humble, or a least tried to be. He decried presumptuousness: "no te quiero consejar,/que paresce presumpción" ("I don't want to advise you, because it appears presumptuous") (I, 187, 86–87), and "sabéis que nuestro Señor/ no quiere la

gente altiva" ("You know that our Lord does not like haughty
people") (I, 198, 67–68). Torres Naharro refers to Rome more than
to any other locality in his poems, and the references are usually
pejorative: "Digo yo, qu'el bien de Roma/ es oylla y nunca vela" ("I
say that the good things about Rome are better to be heard than
seen") (I, 164, 118–19). The dislike of Rome extends by association
to all of Italy as "siempre Italia fue llamada/d'españoles sepoltura"
("Italy was always called a tomb for Spaniards") (I, 194, 81–82).

II Historical Significance

During this period Italy was ravaged by wars resulting from His-
pano-Gallic rivalry. Except for love, war receives most of Torres
Naharro's attention in his poetry. The military information and allusions in his verses are significant for two reasons: first, they provide
a historical background to the poetry and sometimes allow it to be
dated. Some historical references giving an indication for its composition of the *ab quo* variety are seen in the *Capítulo VII*, which
names the statue Laocoön unearthed in 1516 on the Esquiline.
Upon its discovery, Pope Julius had it placed in the Belvedere
Palace of the Vatican. *Epístola VII* mentions Pope Leo X as succes-
sor to Julius II (I, 203, 107); Leo X reigned from 1513 to 1521. There
is no mention of Charles V of Spain (1516–1556), but there is mention of the death of King Fernando (1516), likewise of Gonzalo Fernández de Córdoba (d. 1515), and of duque de Nájera (d. 1515). The
second reason, significant for his poetry, is that the military information and allusions prove that Torres Naharro had a deep knowledge
of military life, probably gained through personal experience. He
not only names the military leaders, but notes battles with their
troop movements, weapons, casualties, and even booty. Such commentary argues considerable military experience. The fact that he
dedicated the *Propalladia* to Fernando Francisco de Ávalos, marqués de Pescara,[2] and husband of Vittoria Colonna, again shows that
Torres Naharro was not alien to those active in the military life.

In the *Psalmo* (*Psalm*) Torres Naharro names the following military leaders: Remón de Cardona, Próspero Colonna, Diego García
de Paredes, Captain Hernando de Alarcón, and the marqués de
Pescara. In the *Retracto* (*Portrait*) he names the marqués de Cález,
the marqués de Villena; in the *Capítulo V* he cites Gonzalo Fernández de Córdoba, the "Gran Capitán" who fought with the forces of
the Holy League and won the Battle of Ceriñola (Chirinola) in 1503

against the French. *Romance I* laments the death of King Fernando
(1516). The same poem also contains a reference to the king's son,
Prince Juan (I, 219, 116), heir to the throne and praised by all who
knew him, who died at the age of nineteen in 1497. A grandchild,
Don Miguel, is also mentioned in Torres Naharro's poetry (I, 219,
121). This child, like the ill-fated Prince Juan before him, might
have crowned the unification of Spain had he not died in 1500. King
Fernando, besides the duque de Nájera, stands out as one of the
most eulogized persons in the works of Torres Naharro.

The language of much of the poetry is that of traditional courtly
love, the vocabulary for which had been established in Spain by the
poets of the *Cancionero* ("Songbook") in the fifteenth century. Love
is courtly, aristocratic, sad, and Platonic, influenced not only by the
Cancionero but also by the works of Petrarch. This Petrarchan vein
is exemplified in the oppositions and contrasts that the poet uses in
the three Italian sonnets written by him in imitation of the Petrarchan form. The *Sátyra* ("Satire") reveals the same interest in oppositions and contrasts: "el mal va por bien, el ayre por muro,/ lo negro
por blanco, lo turbio por claro" ("evil passes for good, air for a wall,
black for white, and muddled for lucid") (I, 158, 97–98).

Even though he spent much of his time in Italy, Torres Naharro
did not do much experimenting with Italian poetic metres. He concentrated his versification primarily on four types. As in the drama,
he preferred to write verses in the octosyllabic couplet with a short-
ened line or broken foot, arranged in strophes of five to seven lines.
He would also use a strophe of twelve octosyllabic lines, a peculiar
combination of his own which he used only in the *Comedia Jacinta*.
For the *Comedia Ymenea* he used a variation of this form with
twelve octosyllabic lines to the strophe, but with the next to the last
line as a broken foot. Along with the couplets of broken foot, he also
used the traditional doubled *redondilla* ("roundelay")—four octosyllabic lines to a strophe with the rhyme *a b b a*. In the *Diálogo
del nascimiento*, he tried the unusually long line of twelve syllables
with ten lines to the strophe, with the short verse or broken foot of
six syllables occurring in the first and sixth lines. In his short poems
he preferred the couplets with broken foot and would essay briefly
into other variables including the satirical dodecasyllabic lines, the
ballad form, the popular song, and the sonnet, the last of which he
wrote only in Italian.[3] Besides Patrarch (1304–1374), another great
poet who had tremendous influence on Torres Naharro's thinking

was Jorge Manrique (1440–1479). The first lines of the *Retracto* are reminiscent of the *Coplas* ("Couplets") of Jorge Manrique on the death of his father, but Torres Naharro's lines do not carry the same strength conveyed in the marked funeral rhythm of Manrique's great poem.

Torres Naharro's poetry did not leave genuine traces in other poets, but it constitutes a document for sixteenth-century life, and, to some extent, a mirror of his own life and personality. His brief versified works deal with the typical topics of unrequited love, satire of pernicious human foibles, adoration of religious figures, and eulogies of political, military, and state leaders. At times he seems intensely personal, and perhaps because of this he was not very receptive to Italian influences. His short poems lack subjective lyricism; in fact, his most lyrical verses are to be found in his *comedias a fantasia* ("fictional comedies")[4] in which paradoxically he can not be too personal; in effect, he is compelled to prevaricate, to speak other's imagined words. Here he escapes from his own emotions into the freedom of sublimated words, forms, and rhythms that soar on to awaken a sympathetic chord in the reader. Both in his poetry and drama, Torres Naharro was "an ardent patriot, a pungent satirist," but above all, as Gillet and Green aptly put it, he was a "dramatist unmatched in the observation of manners, and the unquestioned master of the romantic comedy before Lope de Vega" (IV, 406).

CHAPTER 3

Diálogo Del Nascimiento *and* Addición Del Diálogo

IN our discussion of the stage productions by Torres Naharro we follow the chronological sequence of composition currently accepted. The first combination of plays that Torres Naharro contributed to Spanish belles lettres followed ritual patterns established by the Salamancan school of playwrights. After the summary of the play below, we scrutinize some of these traditional structural patterns.

I *Synopsis*

A young shepherd greets his youthful, agitated audience which he urges forthwith to calm down. He informs spectators that they will see a play the like of which has not been seen in at least a couple of years. He then recounts an adventure with a young lass, whom he pursued for a while, but who managed to escape him. Later, spotting her at a wedding, he sends a salacious note, to which she responds by suggesting a meeting at an upcoming wedding, while cautioning him to beware lest her father see them together. At the wedding he dutifully searches her out, only to be ridiculed, yet, with the help of her cousin, the naive rustic is trapped into marriage with her. Reconciled to the idea, he recites her dowry: a calf, a steer with a bell, a mattress, two chickens, a rooster, a cat and a dog, and even a saddled donkey. He will accept her despite having been told that the sexton has been to bed with her. At this point the shepherd recalls his original mission, which is to tell the audience about the two-part story to be performed. Its theme is a brief exchange of news about Spain, and the miraculous mysteries entailed in the birth of Christ. The prologuist requests silence under threat of curses from the saints of his calendar; he departs, and the performance begins.

Patrispano, a Castilian, is returning from a pilgrimage to Jerusalem, so weary he can hardly move. He wonders when he may

28

finally rest in his tomb. He notes that the blessed night is upon him; it is a great night, brighter than day. When he decides to bed down at the foot of a fountain, another pilgrim, Betiseo, interrupts him. Betiseo, a Spaniard, has just experienced an attack by thieves, who took his winebag, a loss which prompts him to condemn his attackers to die of thirst. Patrispano consoles him, producing his own winebag which contains enough wine for both. Their thoughts turn to philosophical matters as Patrispano finds solace in the Christian belief that the unfortunate will be rewarded by attaining everlasting glory.

The two pilgrims then exchange information of their journeys. Betiseo left Santiago five months ago. When Patrispano wonders how things are in Spain, Betiseo informs him that the land is replete with everything. Moreover, the glorious king and his good people have gained epic victories over the French. In this age, says Betiseo, there is the greatness of deeds, while in other ages there was that of language and of pens. Patrispano expresses the people's longing for peace, but no peace is in sight even at this Christmastime. Recalling that all creatures showed recognition of the importance of Christ's birth, Patrispano describes the familiar manger scene and explains the mystery of the Trinity to Betiseo, as well as biblical events centered on the life of Christ.

After an hour of conversation the two pilgrims decide to continue their journey to Rome. Betiseo informs Patrispano that the Spaniards now have a hospital in Rome, and the two plan to see the many Christian relics in Rome, including the wings of St. Gabriel, a jacket of the Holy Spirit, and some chest armor from St. Michael. In Rome Betiseo plans to buy souvenirs, a confessional, and an Agnus Dei. The two fellow travelers commence their departure, singing a *romance* ("ballad"), *Triste 'staua el padre Adam* (*Sad was Father Adam*), which dwells on the biblical activities of Christmas day and on the significance for man of Christ's birth.

As the *Diálogo del nascimiento* (*Christmas Dialogue*) is concluding, the *Addición del diálogo* (*Addition to the Dialogue*) begins. Just as Patrispano and Betiseo are leaving the stage, two other shepherds, Herrando and Garrapata, call after them. Herrando has just learned that God has been born in little skirts. Betiseo attempts to correct him, which begins an argument. Herrando, with a play on words, cleverly maintains that the Child was born in his mother's skirts. Herrando further claims that Christ was born with a sword and a shield, clarifying this figure of speech by explaining that the shield stands for patience and the sword for justice. Cleverness continues in repartee between Herrando and Garrapata and in questions and answers on the meaning of Christ's birth. Then follow *pullas* ("debasing witticisms") between Herrando and Garrapata.[1] Garrapata asks why the birth of Christ is celebrated now, when only last year they were crying over his death. The four agree to go to midnight mass, whereupon Garrapata wonders what they will say to the abbot once they get there. Herrando offers more witticisms and extends them to various church types like the sexton, vicar, priest, acolyte, curate, and chaplain, making them the hopeless objects of misfortunes, illnesses, obscene comments, and the like. What will Herrando say to more common men? He wishes all sorts of plagues and unfaithful wives upon them. About women? Women should come to him and to his friends to get their fun. All agree to let Patrispano sing in Latin while Betiseo will sing in *romance* (in the Roman fashion, that is, in the vernacular) a hymn in praise of the Virgin, *Ave Maris Stella* (*Hail Star of the Sea*), and as each line is sung in macaronic Latin, Herrando parodies it with incongruous Spanish words suggested by the sounds of the Latin ones.

II *Analysis*

This first extant dramatic production composed by Torres Naharro consists of three parts, a preface or *introito* ("introit"), the *Christmas Dialogue* and the *Addition to the Dialogue*, this arrangement suggesting a structure similar to that of a triptych. The center piece of devotional interest is flanked by adjacent scenes of jolly fun. Counting all three parts of it, the work has 1,111 lines, approximating the length of one act of the later three-act dramas of the Golden Age (the period of Spanish belles lettres stretching from 1550 to about 1700). The piece was composed when Torres Naharro had already arrived on Italian soil sometime after 1503. Gillet conjectures its composition date to be between 1505 and 1507 (IV, 479).

Both parts of the play were probably recited as a single unit at Christmastime either at one or at two sittings of the audience, that is, with a possible intermission between the two acts. The *Addición*, as its title makes clear, is just a part of the longer work. The combined form was evidently performed prior to its publication, because the prologuist announces the performance of both parts on the same occasion. Possibly, however, the *Diálogo* was composed and presented first, around 1505, and the *Addición* appended to it two years later, together with a rewritten or newly composed introit and *argumento* ("argument" or "plot summary"). We really do not know the sequence of composition, but perhaps when Torres Naharro decided to add the *Addición*, he also hit upon the device of the introit, a forerunner of which was used by Lucas Fernández and which Torres Naharro noticed being used in the Italian drama and to some extent in the ancient Roman plays then being presented.[2]

Although Torres Naharro constructs this play in the biblical and traditionally pastoral fashion of Juan del Encina and Lucas Fernández, he does innovate to some extent by preceding it with the above-mentioned introit and argument. The playwright himself (probably wearing the garb of a rustic shepherd) emerges to recite the prologue. He begins with a note of social discipline that becomes a characteristic of the author's works, cautioning the people to behave; the girls must avoid stealing grapes and fruit. He boastfully announces that he knows how to read; he is a *medio gramata* ("half literate"). But his introductory remarks, as in the summary, quickly turn to the subject of woman. The Renaissance was socially permissive, and this was reflected in its literature. Torres Naharro's audience was not shocked by sexual or scatological comments. The rustic openly confesses his temptations, and in the fashion of the shepherds of Lucas Fernández, he enumerates a dowry that came along with his bride, a recitation that harks back to Juan Ruiz's *serranillas* ("mountain girl songs") in the *Libro de buen amor (Book of Good Love)* (1330). The dowry episode befits a play prepared to celebrate a marriage.[3] This two-part play probably celebrated both a wedding and Christmas festivities.

It was in the circle of Juan del Encina (1469?–1529) and his disciples, notable among whom were Lucas Fernández (1474–1542) and Gil Vicente (1465?–1537?), that Bartolomé de Torres Naharro acquired, in the fashion of an apprentice, the trade of the actor-dramatist. These four playwrights constituted what came to be known as the Salamancan school of dramatists. Torres Naharro's Salamancan mentor, Encina, left his native land around 1498 and emigrated first to Portugal and then proceeded on to Italy to seek his fortune among the Spanish immigrants there. In due time Torres Naharro also succumbed to the call of adventure, fame, and fortune offered by Italy. His first theatrical attempt was composed in the pattern established earlier by the eclogues of Encina and to some

extent by the farces of Lucas Fernández.[4] He was not at this point a
pioneer in making the Christmas eclogue largely theological and
discursive, because Lucas Fernández had already composed and
presented several of his semireligious farces by 1502 along these very
lines.[5] If it had not been for Lucas Fernández's example in the
Égloga o farsa del nascimiento (*Eclogue or Farce of the Nativity*)
(1500) in which Lucas Fernández introduces the character of the
hermit Macario, Torres Naharro probably would not have introduced the character of Patrispano. Macario (model for Patrispano)
comes upon the shepherds, Bonifacio and Gil, in Lucas Fernández's
play and enlightens them concerning the mysteries of redemption.
Similarly, Bonifacio's embryonic boastful qualities are emulated by
the introit speaker in this initial play of Torres Naharro.

The Christmas play, capitalizing on the presence of the shepherds
and the manger scene, was a popular form of entertainment in
Europe during the late medieval and Renaissance periods. In England, for example, it is preserved in the Towneley Cycle of the
fourteenth century. In Spain, as Gillet and Green remind us, this
type of theological and didactic play later "found favor with Diego
Sánchez de Badajoz, Montemayor, Timoneda, and López de
Úbeda, and in the seventeenth century was expanded and incorporated into the *autos* (sacramental one-act plays) of the school of
Calderón" (IV, 561). Although both the secular and religious theater
had a long history, by quirk of fate Torres Naharro began his career
by writing on a religious, rather than on a secular topic. Nevertheless, he borrowed from the tradition of both the popular and secular
theater, incorporating elements of each into his presentation commemorating the Christmas event and a wedding celebration.

The rustic of the introit, speaking the peculiar jargon called
Sayaqués,[6] introduces the two pilgrims, Patrispano and Betiseo. A
typical formulaic device in the Torres Naharro prologue is exercised
here: the speaker forgets his mission and then suddenly recalls his
purpose, which is to recount the story. Before the rustic exits, he
asks that close attention be given to the action which is to take place.

The opening remarks of the introit to this shortest of Torres
Naharro's plays are paradoxically longer than for some of his fuller
plays. This prologue is longer, for example, than the preface (84
lines) to the *Comedia Jacinta* (1301 lines), and equals with its 99
lines the prefatory remarks (99 lines) of the *Comedia Soldadesca*

life of ease, while
provides his own
d to discreet par-
he use of "whips
finer adults than
, the poor will be
ked, leisure class

us discussion of
the *Addición*. As
cal and religious
riddles on geog-
citation of *pullas*
urch.
gh the works of
previous deflora-
e naive husband
the clergy occurs
t's birth. Despite
. Life, according
, slips away irre-

earlier, Torres
ially against the
(Chirinola) and
1503, and De-
e Great Captain
rom the prover-
t military leader,
Diálogo, discus-
aharro shows an
st the French in
omplishment of
Aeneid of Virgil
destruction had
r and ingenuity

nts which were
s of troops, the

r with the *Addición* is ap-
s created earlier by Encina
n according to the number
or the *Addición*, and thirty
ollows the introit's 99 lines.
the *Diálogo* by itself was
dience was normally accus-
performances, and probably
ncreased the play's length
y fifty percent. This early
nt preferences marked the
ip important in all of Torres

d in Italy from Spain under-
nd that he expresses in the
ts in the audience. Can the
dhood ever fade away? This
Patrispano, on a journey to
eo happily relates the events
out his work Torres Naharro
the voluntary or involuntary
empting to fill their insatiable

e guise of the shepherd, it is
me out again as one of the
Gillet seems to identify with
etiseo, who comes from San-
ure appears to be an Andalu-
h Torres Naharro was proba-
n of the play, the *Diálogo*. In
taken by Torres Naharro (as-
vas probably that of Herrando

on his world and observations
. When Betiseo relates his un-
which he would have preferred
e, he receives sympathy from
ian virtues and offers to share
fortunate companion. He won-

ders aloud how it is that the wicked are granted a
many good people have to suffer incessantly. He
answer to the socio-religious theme, likening G
ents who teach their children to mind through
rather than gifts." Punishment and suffering mol
does a life of ease (I, 268, 135–39). Consequentl
assured a heavenly life, while it will fall to the wi
to undergo the trials of afterlife.

In the *Diálogo* Torres Naharro offers a seri
theological problems, while emphasizing humor i
the play progresses, the exchange of philosoph
questions and answers turns into an exchange o
raphy, science, and cosmology, terminating in a 1
aimed at specific types of people related to the c

Satire of the clergy is a theme that runs thro
Torres Naharro. In the prologue, the rustic bride's
tion by a sexton is supposedly a real advantage for t
since "the man finds her experienced." Satire of
when mention is made of their ingratitude at Chris
the clerical criticism, religion is devoutly supporte
to the primary message of this semireligious piec
trievably unless there is faith in redemption.

With the nostalgic pride in Spain mentione
Naharro acclaims Spain's victories in Italy, espe
French. Decisive battles—the Battles of Ceriñol
Garigliano (Garellano)—were fought on April 28
cember 28, 1503, respectively. In both of these, ti
Gonzalo Fernández de Córdoba snatched victory
bial jaws of defeat. Torres Naharro praises this grea
the Cordobés, for his conquests in Italy, and in the
sing the greatness of Spain and its king, Torres N
inclination to write an epic of the Spanish wars agai
Italy (I, 271, 215–19). He is convinced that the ac
the Spaniards would overshadow those sung in the
and in the *Pharsalia* of Lucan. Man's power of
become so vast that a corresponding growth in val
was needed to survive the calamity of war.

Torres Naharro was aware of the radical elem
beginning to transform warfare: the larger masse

beginning of standing armies, the more disciplined military formations, the new firearms, the greater complexity in tactics, and the more elaborate engineering feats. In this play, as in others, Torres Naharro protests against firearms and scientific inventions in general. He notes where armaments are manufactured, aware that Milan, Italy, was the center of the weapons industry, and names Espluch (otherwise known as Innsbruck) which was recognized in the Renaissance for its famous artillery pieces. The military importance of Innsbruck was exploited from the time of the Romans when their legions made it a center for their own defenses, armaments, and operations (I, 271, 241).

Gillet ventures that the *Diálogo* is a combination of a Christmas play and a political peace play like Francisco de Madrid's *Égloga* (1494) on the invasion of Italy by Charles VIII of France (IV, 554, n. 1). When Torres Naharro's Patrispano calls for a stop to wars, or at least a stop to their exaltation, Erasmus had not yet written his *Querrela pacis (Complaint of Peace)*. Torres Naharro deplores the warfare between Christians and the pope's aid of one side or another. The oft-repeated yearning for peace at Christmas, of all times in the year, finds open expression in the playlet (I, 272, 257).

Torres Naharro in his remarks on a new epic shows familiarity with the Roman cultural tradition and its great writers, Virgil and Lucan. Lucan had exercised considerable influence on Juan de Mena and Íñigo López de Mendoza. And, of course, the Spanish language was now deemed just as sophisticated as Latin had been, and therefore it was ripe for further literary epic productions. But Torres Naharro appears never to have realized his dream of writing a new Spanish epic commemorating the nation's military victories in Italy.

At the conclusion of the *Addición*, Betiseo calls for a repetition of the ballad that ended the preceding *Diálogo*, but Patrispano disagrees and leads them in singing a Latin hymn with a refrain "Celorum via/ nobilis est Maria" ("Mary is the way of noble heaven"). There follows a burlesquing of the hymn with a play on the words Eva-Ave, where the reversal of the name mirrors the conversion of sin to redemption. The interlineal farcing of the hymn is in a popular, medieval vein, incongruous, grotesque, and close to irreverent. This final song, a mixture of the sacred and the profane, has the effect of combining the religious faith and the festival spirit of Christmas Eve into one musical expression. The song is in six and five syllable lines with mingled irregular, assonantal, and consonantal rhyme.

Offering a general appraisal of the play, Green wrote:

> To me it seems that the occasion—a joyous gathering of the Spanish colony in Rome on Christmas Eve to await the *misa del gallo* (midnight mass)—did not call for a serious attack on Church abuse. Rome, on this joyous evening, was the Eternal City, filled with relics and wonders (even though some of these are gently burlesqued). It was not, on this particular night, a school of sin, nor a paradise of lechery. It was, rather, at this particular moment the spiritual home of the expatriated Extremaduran (Torres Naharro) and of those for whom he sought to provide, during an hour or two before the *misa del gallo*, a sense both of reverent awareness, of the origins of their religion, and of carefree rejoicing in the thought that somehow the Redemption must redeem the world. (IV, 560)

Green continues, "Here once more we have a *Gelegenheitsstück* (play of occasion) that admirably fulfills its purpose and that certainly must have been applauded . . . [in its time by the youths] who had followed Spain's star of empire to the sister Peninsula" (IV, 561).

On versification, Menéndez y Pelayo observed that the dodecasyllabic verse that Torres Naharro used for the *Diálogo* is his own invention, and that it was later used by Gil Vicente.[7] The stanza has the *quintilla* ("five line") rhyme, *a a b a b* , in which the first line of each stanza consists of only six syllables. For the *Addición*, however, Torres Naharro modified the stanzaic form by shortening the broken line to four syllables and using the traditional line of eight syllables for the rest of the *quintilla*. These five-line stanzas appeared frequently in the early theater, although in the shorter eight-syllable line, rather than in the twelve syllables Torres Naharro used in the *Diálogo*. Torres Naharro's essay into the longer twelve syllable line for the drama was short-lived. After the *Diálogo* he preferred to use a version of the eight, nine or ten syllable line of the *quintilla*. In sum, the *Diálogo* and *Addición* unit composed in the manner of the Salamancan school of playwrights is a semireligious piece of drama for a merry group gathered on a relaxed religious occasion, temporarily removed from the seriousness of an incensed religious political atmosphere.

Much of the play is just plain earthy fun, while some of it, to be sure, has theological intent and moments of inspiring devotion. The

Diálogo and its *Addición* are noteworthy for the liveliness of the dialogue. The author is fully aware that this, rather than dramatic conflict, is its chief attribute. A variety of themes and opinions exchanged among the speakers of the play is based on the recognition of each individual's worth and on the validity of varied opinions, deeply rooted in human purposes. Only one thesis is upheld: that redemption is brought through Christ, and it is His birth that Torres Naharro here joyously commemorates. He thus inaugurates his profession as a dramatist in the traditional way with the Christmas play of the *Diálogo*, but begins to try out his comic talent in the *Addición*, which tends in the direction of a marriage play. After this decisive transition from religious to profane comedy, with the added influence of the sophisticated Italian humanistic theater, he emerges to set the pace for a new type of secular Spanish comedy, pursued successfully for the rest of his career as a playwright. We shall see the basic principles and the pattern for this success in the following chapters.

Following initiation into the company of Spanish playwrights with this unified pair of Christmas-marriage plays, Torres Naharro set out on a more inventive course that led him in two significant paths, one to the *comedia a fantasía* ("fictional comedy") and the other to the *comedia a noticia* ("documentary play"). The realm of the fictional comedy with a wholly invented plot (a plot that strains the sphere of the credible yet remains within the bounds of the humanly imaginable) attracts the dramatist for his next work.

CHAPTER 4

Comedia Seraphina

HAVING tried and proved his talent for the stage, Torres
Naharro turns aside from the ritualistically conditioned material to explore a completely different form which offers a chance to
escape the stark realism of life without rejecting it entirely, and
embraces in its phantasy a world of harmony that brings a comforting, ordered existence. But even this is not without its difficult
moments spent combating the perplexing obstacles cast in life's way
which hinder and challenge its purposes. The *Comedia Seraphina*
(*The Seraphic Comedy*, 1508–1509) is the first of Torres Naharro's
group of fictional comedies.

I *Synopsis*

The rustic shepherd greets his honored audience in the Sayagués
dialect desiring everything good for Christmas and the New Year.
He boasts of how well he can meet and greet people while others are
unable to do so, and speaks of erotic pursuit of a girl who grabs a
cudgel and proceeds to give him a thrashing. He remembers his
mission but in his absentmindedness turns to boasting of his rustic
prowess in jumping, dancing, and making spoons and of his ability to
leaf through missal and baptismal books. A second erotic lapse concerns an attack on another rustic girl who also rejects him. His
attention is turned once again to his mission, and he relates the plot
of the five-act comedy act by act—necessary because the play is
difficult to understand. Close attention is required since the characters speak four different languages: Latin, Italian, Castilian, and
Valencian. The prologuist then calls the company of players, promising the spectators, almost as a threat, that all of them will be
pleased, lest the abbot cast his malediction upon them.

Act 1 opens with Dorosía, maid of Seraphina, desperately
searching for Floristán. They have just learned after Seraphina and

38

Floristán's betrothal that Floristán has already been married and
that he is therefore a bigamist. Clever Lenicio, Floristán's
confidant, attempts to defend his master's actions. Lenicio exhibits
loving designs on Dorosía, but so does a rival, Gomecio (a fool of a
scholar), servant of the hypocritical hermit, Teodoro. Lenicio hopes
to turn a profit from Gomecio's love of Dorosía. When Gomecio sees
Dorosía, he expresses his love for her in macaronic Latin. Dorosía
rejects him while casting aspersions on men's fidelity. When Teodoro appears, he and Gomecio speak in Latin about their interest in
women, and the scene ends with disgruntled Teodoro beating
Gomecio and running him off the stage. In the next scene Lenicio
and Floristán recapitulate: Floristán has promised to marry
Seraphina and, moreover, she has allowed him to consummate their
promise to marry. Although she has submitted to him sexually, she
likes her independence and refuses to cohabit with him on a regular
basis. Floristán's father is responsible for arranging his first marriage
by proxy to an Italian girl, Orphea. Lenicio advises Floristán that
Orphea is actually better suited for him than is Seraphina, but
Floristán decides to stay true to his Seraphina, his only real love.

Floristán's steadfast love for Seraphina is bolstered by his
confidence that he will extricate himself from the dilemma with his
official wife, Orphea, remedy his situation, and marry Seraphina. To
help him resolve the love triangle, Floristán expects advice from the
hermit Teodoro. Left alone on stage, Lenicio terminates the act
philosophically by noting that his master is an ass for being a
bigamist. He concludes that one woman is enough and observes the
three things to beware of: an unlearned doctor, an indigent alchemist, and a fat cleric.

Seraphina, namesake of the play, appears in the first scene of the
second act to recapitulate her predicament. Teodoro, after exchanging pleasantries, advises her to have faith. In her following
scene with Dorosía, Seraphina tells Dorosía that she will love Floristán forever, suggesting that the only way to correct this wrong he
has committed is to have his other wife Orphea killed. Meantime,
Seraphina scorns Floristán, even though he threatens suicide.
When she proposes that he kill Orphea, Floristán agrees to do so
within the hour. When Seraphina next speaks with Lenicio, he
falsely tells her that Orphea is an impoverished, homely woman.
Lenicio enlists Seraphina's cooperation in playing a trick on
Gomecio when he attempts to further his love for Dorosía.

Act 3 begins with a recapitulation of the preceding two acts by Floristán. He fell in love and "married" Seraphina, a Valencian, but according to his father's forceful wishes, was married by proxy to Orphea, an Italian girl. He feels he should kill himself, but does not want to. He reasons, as he has also been urged to do by others, that he should kill Orphea where Seraphina can see him do it, so she can believe the deed has been done, and they will then be free to marry. He can not kill himself, he claims, because this would plunge his beloved Seraphina into despair (earlier, however, she had told him he should have killed himself before he came to see her). He falsely rationalizes that Orphea would not be able to live without him either. While Floristán laments the unfortunate state of women, Bruneta, a servant of Orphea, approaches him.

Bruneta in a soliloquy denounces the deceiving ways of men, noting that if Orphea really wanted to, she could marry her old flame, Floristán's handsomer brother, Policiano. Floristán seeks out Orphea with intentions to kill her. When he tells her to confess, she wants to know why she must die. Hearing his explanation of bigamy, she disclaims any sense of guilt. If she dies, all will mourn her: men, women, the earth, the sea, and the animals. She asks pardon only if she has not loved him and served him well. Floristán assures her that her real happiness lies in the life beyond the grave, while his fate will be to remain alive and suffer. Orphea asks that a tombstone be erected to proclaim her noble life and death. Bruneta requests to die with her mistress, but suddenly, Floristán passionately relents. Orphea is permitted to live; instead, he wishes to bring death upon himself, and slips into a philosophical inquiry on the meaning of life. Why was he given a soul? Why did he survive his birth? His benumbed existence is as if his body were in the grave and his soul already in hell.

In act 4 Lenicio offers yet another recapitulation of the story, and curses both Teodoro, for poorly advising Floristán, and Gomecio, for competing with him for Dorosía's love. When Gomecio appears, Lenicio begins to implement his practical joke, telling him to kiss Dorosía in the presence of her mistress. To conjure up Dorosía's love, he ties Gomecio's thumbs together and articulates macaronic Latin for magic effect. When Teodoro comes, he finds Gomecio thus bound looking imploringly to heaven. In disgust he frees Gomecio and sends him home with another beating. Meanwhile, Lenicio from a distance laughs gleefully. Continuing with his picaresque behavior, he decides to tell Dorosía that Orphea is dead. Seraphina, now with Dorosía, believes the report of Orphea's death to be true, but suffers doubts now about marrying a murderer. After all, Floristán may murder her, as he did Orphea. Gomecio, acting upon Lenicio's advice, plants a kiss on Dorosía, whereupon he is attacked by both women, and is rescued only by the timely intervention of his master Teodoro. When Floristán returns to see Seraphina, she still persists in her scornful ways. Frustrated and disillusioned, he decides to return to Orphea. At this point Bruneta rushes out to tell him that Orphea has fainted. Teodoro concludes the act with a Latin hymn pondering the meaning of life and death and praising the Virgin.

Act 5 opens with Lenicio's announcement that Floristán's handsome brother, Policiano, has returned home a wealthy man. Just three years ago he had been Orphea's lover and had disappeared. Teodoro, aware of Policiano's return, realizes the potential solution: Floristán can take Seraphina for a wife, and Policiano, unless he has married during his three year absence, can marry Orphea, since she, unlike Seraphina, has remained a virgin. Yet, Floristán is haunted by the idea that if Orphea lives, he still can not marry Seraphina. He is finally assured by Teodoro that divine grace annuls an unconsummated marriage.

Seraphina appears in a portal to divulge her fear that Floristán will kill her, as he did Orphea. Enlightened as to the new turn of events, she eagerly accepts Floristán for her husband. But now there is talk of war, and Floristán plans to join the armed forces, expecting to enrich himself by becoming a captain. He muses of how in war, by threatening the peasants with beatings and death, the soldiers always get what they want, including women. The awaited reunion between the brothers, Policiano and Floristán, joyously takes place. Policiano reports his years of grief spent in pining for his unnamed secret love, threatening to undo the satisfactory ending already planned. The suspenseful delaying moments are happily concluded when the name of his secret love is pried from his lips: Orphea. The pieces of the puzzle fall in place. Teodoro recites the play's closing lines in Latin. The journey of the day is ended, there will be a multiple wedding, and now, all that remains is applause from the audience and a farewell from the actors.

II *Analysis*

Coming after the two-part *Diálogo del nascimiento* and its *Addición*, this is the longest, and earliest, of the five-act plays that Torres

Naharro published in his first edition of the *Propalladia* (1517).[1]
Together with its introit and argument the drama numbers 2536
lines. These are written in a combination of two *redondillas*, with
octosyllabic lines that rhyme *a b b a a c c a*. Perhaps partly because
of its length, J. P. W. Crawford believed this to be the last one of the
plays prepared for the 1517 publication. He estimated the date for
the work's composition as 1515. Nevertheless, he felt that, despite
its length, it was not one of Torres Naharro's exceptionally good
plays.[2]

In his discussion of the play's chronology, Gillet hazards an earlier
date for its composition, considering the play to have been written
after the *Diálogo del nascimiento* (1505–1507), and before the *Comedia Soldadesca* (1510). Thereby Gillet deduces the period of composition as 1508–1509, simply on the evidence that the play's locale
is Valencia, whereas the locale of the *Comedia Soldadesca* is the city
of Rome (IV, 473). Since Torres Naharro is presumed to have lived
in Valencia before he embarked for Rome, it seems to Gillet that the
sequence of the plays should follow the sequence of Torres
Naharro's experience. This argument, while not perfectly convincing, does have its merits. The *Seraphina*, like the *Soldadesca*, was
probably composed on Italian, rather than on Spanish soil, and first
produced for Spanish emigrés living in Rome and Naples: the audience was international in outlook and comprised of heterogeneous
ethnic elements from the two cities. The *Seraphina* was composed
for a liguistically hospitable audience, sectors of which were fluent
in Castilian, Italian, Valencian,and Latin. These languages were
extensively used throughout the play in their standard as well as in
their nonstandard dialectal forms. Alongside the correct Latin,
there appeared likewise a corrupted macaronic version of it.

The *Comedia Seraphina*, a *comedia a fantasia* (fictional comedy),
is classified as a marriage play, that is, written most probably to
celebrate a wedding. But it could have been used on almost any gala
occasion, even on a church holiday to entertain the multilingual
portions of the populace of Rome and Naples. It seems to have been
performed originally around Christmas time and the New Year since
the introit speaker greets his audience with a wish for prosperity:
"Mil buenas pascuas ayáis/ y otros tantos años buenos" ("May you
have a thousand good Christmases, and as many good years") (II, 3,
1–2). This internal evidence can not be taken too seriously, however, because it is entirely possible that such an expression as we

have here can be used incongruously by the brazenly bold shepherd to produce a humorous effect on the audience at any given time of the year. Although the *Seraphina* may have had its debut in Rome or Naples, the locale of the play's action itself is Valencia, and the scene is designated as a street of that Spanish coastal city. The seaport city, like Rome, was a melting pot, reflecting the mixed but close ethnic relationship between the two Romance peninsulas. Many Castilians on their way to embark for Italy would remain in the city for a while, and among those of marrying age, there would naturally develop liaisons with counterparts of other nationalities.

The *Seraphina* is an urban comedy, a radical change from the earlier pastoral play on the Bethlehem scene. Torres Naharro remembers certain familiar sights of Valencian landmarks, the busy church of Saint Agostí, and the terrifying gallows of Carraxet, mentioning also the notorious Valencian seaport's red-light district. The overall atmosphere, superbly Valencian, is underscored by the consistent, authentic use of the Valencian version of the Catalan language by both the heroine and her maid.[3] Along with the Valencian geographical allusions, there is also the mention of Seville, to which Torres Naharro later may have moved after leaving Italy (II, 73, 202), and reference likewise to Rome and its river, the Tiber.

Because of the diversity of languages and dialects spoken in the play, the drama is not easy to comprehend. As noted, Seraphina, and Dorosía speak only in Valencian. Floristán, Policiano, and Lenicio speak in Castilian; Orphea and Bruneta converse in Italian; while Latin is preferred by Teodoro and his servant Gomecio. Due to this multilingual dialogue, many of the puns, much of the humor, and the subtle nuances of language can be lost to the audience and to the reader who may be unfamiliar with the various languages represented by the dialogue. Gillet, who spent a lifetime on Torres Naharro's plays, confesses on several occasions the inability to catch the meaning of certain of its expressions (III, 230, n.40; 281, n.200). We may suspect that even Torres Naharro's melting pot audience was not expected to recognize and enjoy, all at once, the linguistic intricacies contained in the text.

The Italian spoken by Orphea in the *Comedia Seraphina* is of the northern variety found in Sienna and Florence. On occasion it does share traits with some southern speech forms as well (III, 283, n.311). At least part of the audience which Torres Naharro entertained was evidently learned, inasmuch as it was expected to understand the story in scenes written entirely in Latin. Besides this play, the *Tinellaria* and the *Soldadesca* also include dialogues in languages other than Spanish.

Even though the Greek word "drama" etymologically means "action," the essence of drama, as we have come to understand the meaning of the term today, generally is not simply action, but rather action with a conflict. It matters not whether the conflict is internal, that is, psychological, or external, that is, physical. The nature of the conflict is flexible; it can be just as easily ridiculous as it can be serious, tragic, or even sublime. The conflict in the *Comedia Seraphina* can be interpreted in different ways. Some critics consider it a foolish play that was intended to be serious; others think of it as a ridiculously funny play. This only proves that there is no accounting for taste no matter how sophisticated, how pretentious, or for that matter, how naive it may be. Understandably, critical opinion varies on the appraisal of this work. Martínez de la Rosa and Leandro Fernández de Moratín took the *Comedia Seraphina* seriously and scored it by insisting on this interpretation. Conversely, Miguel Romera-Navarro agreed with M. Menéndez y Pelayo that the play was written as a jest.[4] Gillet agrees with Menéndez y Pelayo's interpretation that this was a jocular work. In fact, when Gomecio receives a beating from Teodoro and is slapped by Seraphina after stealthily kissing Dorosîa, the play shifts from a comfortably pleasant situation comedy to the casual cruelty of a slapstick farce. The play can be enjoyed as a *bufonada* ("jest") despite some shortcomings of dramatic technique. Basically, it is a sound comedy although vulnerable to misinterpretation. Its multilingual aspect, obscuring much of the humor, makes it the most difficult of Torres Naharro's works for an audience to appreciate in its entirety.

The play is notable for the depiction of parallel loves on different respective levels between masters and servants. Floristán and Seraphina are depicted on one level and Lenicio, Gomecio, and Dorosía on another. Orphea constitutes the third party in the eternal triangle on the upper level, while Teodoro is the superfluous lover of Dorosía on the lower level.

This play does not have the visual splendor of the *Comedia Trophea* and with its representation of customs and mores is more in line with other multilingual documentary plays, the *Soldadesca* and *Tinellaria*. Yet, from the standpoint of plot, it does not resemble these documentary plays as much as it does such fictional comedies as the *Calamita, Ymenea,* and the *Aquilana.* All four are developed on the basis of a love affair with an accompanying parody. All have suspense keyed to the threat of violent death, but all end happily with marriage ceremonies.

III *Sources and Influences*

Predictably, the sources for this play are manifold. This *comedia a fantasía* derives its title from the adjectival form of the name of the protagonist, a practice taken from Plautus and Terence and a host of Renaissance humanistic plays of the period.[5] The practice continued in the sixteenth-century Spanish drama with countless works and on through to the present day.

The title of the play and name of the protagonist may have been suggested to Torres Naharro by a memorable individual such as Serafino Aquilano de' Ciminelli dall' Aquila (1466–1500), a famous improvisor, poet, and writer of eclogues, who served Cesare Borgia in the same palace in which Torres Naharro likewise found protection. Two other charactonyms may have come from Poliziano and his work, *Orfeo* (1471). Such names as these with a classical flavor became a traditional tag among the populace, and thus could have emanated from the people as they provided the alert dramatist with some of his material. Another source for Torres Naharro's play includes the traditionally popular proverbs meant to emphasize the ideas and attitudes the author is developing in the various scenes: "piensa engañar a Dios/ y el necio engáñase a sí" ("he thinks to deceive God and the fool only deceives himself") (II, 23, 415–16). Besides many such proverbial expressions, another popular source is traceable to the wisdom emanating from biblical inspiration, as in the case of Floristán's closing soliloquy of act 3 where he finds himself "cercado de planto eterno" ("surrounded by an eternal plaint") (II, 53, 514). This idea is reminiscent of Psalm 18:4, "The sorrows of death compassed me. . . ." Besides common poetic concepts that Torres Naharro utilized: "que muero porque no muero" ("I'm dying because I'm not dying") (II, 77, 344),[6] there are echoes which could suggest Torres Naharro's altogether probable acquaintance with León Hebreo's *Dialoghi d'amore* (ca. 1502) as a foundation for Orphea's plaint (II, 48, 337–68). Floristán's ridiculous courtly love for Seraphina and the ruffianesque love of the servants, as well as the false braggadocio of Lenicio covering his cowardice, recall the varied male characters of *La Celestina,* and of Machiavelli's plays, the *Commedia in versi* and the *Mandragola.* The latter, in particular, offers the character of Fra Timoteo as a point of departure for the creation of the hermit Teodoro. The unconsummated marriage between Orphea and Floristán has its antecedents as far back as the classical work of Terence's *Hecyra.* Much of the technique of the play no doubt comes also from the Renaissance humanistic stage productions that acted upon Torres Naharro's fertile mind. Beyond this, the source of the plot where the protagonist is expected to kill his wife as a test of his own love for another woman, whom thereupon he can marry, is found in a different type of popular tradition, that of the popular ballad, known as *El romance del conde Alarcos (The Ballad of Count Alarcos).*[7]

For the linguistic influences, we may note that Torres Naharro displayed a good knowledge of the Italian language of the north-central region of Tuscany. He already knew Latin, Castilian, and Valencian by the time he arrived in Italy. For the use of Sayagués one can detect an influence of the Salamancan school of dramatists. This influence derives from Lucas Fernández and Juan del Encina. Besides dialectal influences, others of the thematic nature recall the works of the Salamancan school: Policiano complains of love in the same effusive way as do the shepherds of Lucas Fernández in his *Farsas y églogas (Farces and Eclogues,* 1514). Floristán, like the shepherd of Lucas Fernández who suffers unrequited love, undergoes a change, having become a shadow of his former self (II, 52, 505–9). The burlesque of courtly love in the *Comedia Seraphina* is akin to that found in the works of Lucas Fernández and in *La Celestina* of Rojas; but such burlesque was something of a vogue that pervaded the contemporary scene, and its source for Torres Naharro's play need not be sought in any one unique work.

To ascertain the influence that Torres Naharro's work had on others is an equally hazardous and perplexing operation. It is easier to follow the transfer of his ideas to some of his own plays. A presaging element in this drama resurfaces in the author's later work, the *Comedia Soldadesca.* The picture of war that Floristán presents in the last act of the *Seraphina* where he suggests that he might become a captain and make himself rich sets the stage for the Guzmán and his cohorts in the *Comedia Soldadesca,* and for the hapless victimized Italian peasants. The glimpses of wartime life provided by Floristán are put into practice by Torres Naharro's venturesome recruits of the *Soldadesca*. Torres Naharro is on the verge of a successful theatrical formula in his *Seraphina;* reverberations appear notably in the *Calamita*. Both plays open with the rascally servant plotting to take advantage of the town's dunce. While the *Calamita* is technically more sophisticated, the *Seraphina* exhibits greater lyricism. Both possess rudiments of the cape and sword plays of the Golden Age.

Another presaging element in the *Seraphina* is one that heralds a later scene of the superbly structured *Ymenea,* that of the potentially tragic confrontation between the unfortunate female victim and her avowed executioner. In the scene in which Floristán prepares to kill Orphea, he informs her that her hour to die has come. Orphea rises to a self-defense that finds echoes in Phebea's eloquence in the *Ymenea*. Phebea, like Orphea, pleads for her life; then asks pardon only if she has not loved her betrothed faithfully, and, finally, resigned to death, declaims a lament of pathetic fallacy in which she pictures all men, women, and nature joining to mourn her unjust demise (*Seraphina*, II, 46–50; *Ymenea*, II, 312–17).

Torres Naharro helps to propagate and develop the age-old theme of "life is a dream" for the Spanish stage. Floristán, unusually lyrical for his character, plunges into a memorable soliloquy at the close of act 3. Like prince Segismundo in Calderón's *La vida es sueño* (*Life is a Dream*) a century and a half later, he asks rhetorically why he was given a soul, why he was born, when unfortunately he can not have the freedom of action he desires. Floristán elsewhere shows himself to be grotesquely irrational, but with this beautiful soliloquy, the playwright converts him into a sage.

Torres Naharro was a transmitter of ideas, of proverbial expressions, of popular ballad material, and of poetic and philosophical phrases. All of these with his clear and simple style were well appreciated. C. de Villalón writes in glowing terms of Torres Naharro's poetic talent and Juan de Valdés praised his style: "El estilo que tiene Torres Naharro en su *Propalladia* . . . me satisfaze mucho, porque es muy llano y sin afetación ninguna . . ." ("The style that Torres Naharro has in his *Propalladia* satisfies me a lot, because it is plain and without any affectation . . .").[8]

IV   *Structure*

In the opinion of Gillet and Green, this is a well structured play with "its orderly division into acts and the careful linking of its

scenes, the controlled rise of tension toward the end of act 3, and
the judicious distribution of comic relief, [along with] the long
maintenance of suspense" (IV, 489). Menéndez y Pelayo views it
differently and finds it lacking in form. He considers it to be the
least classical of Torres Naharro's full-length plays. From a compara-
tive, dramatic perspective, certainly the *Seraphina* is better structured than the *Trophea*, but not as unified, polished, nor as disciplined as the *Ymenea*. Structurally, it ranks somewhere between
these two.

There are several good technical aspects to the play: prefigurations are skillfully woven into the scheme of the plot leading up to
the climactic scene, and recapitulations appropriately placed to re-
sume and convey the direction of the story at the start of acts
2,3,and 4. Throughout most of the drama, a decreed tragedy haunts
those who have dared to love. The resolution of the plot is sys-
tematized with the artifice of the *deus ex machina*.

There is, nonetheless, a notable lack of continuity for some of the
scenes in which characters meet by sheer coincidence (II, 64). On
the other hand, this can be a very effective contrivance for creating
humorous encounters, even though it does not serve well for serious
purposes. Whether this is a plus or minus in the evaluation of the
piece depends clearly in the final analysis on one's interpretation of
the play's comic or serious intent. Other instances corroborating
good structure include Seraphina's first entrance on stage (II, 70)
and Policiano's arrival prior to the turning point of the play. These
are technically well devised and prepared for. Some scenes, like the
one at the end of the second act, have an effective curtain that leads
on to suspense and a fresh renewal of interest. There is also an
injection of a delaying element which turns out to be deliberately
misleading, but which serves to prolong a suspenseful anticipation
at the climactic point, rewarded by the final agreeable outcome.

V   *Audience Awareness*

We have noticed briefly the play-audience awareness the author
manifests even in his first dramatic effort, the *Diálogo del nascimiento*. What are the instances of the play-audience relationship
evident here? As usual, Torres Naharro begins with the greeting by
the introit speaker to his *gente onrada* ("honored people") (II, 5, 73).
They are informed that the play is hard to follow and are alerted to
the four languages in it. Moreover, the spectators are told that the

fourth act is just a *jornadeta* ("a short day's trip," that is , "a brief act"), and the play will have a happy ending. Throughout the play the dramatist makes a calculated effort to keep the audience informed of the progressing action. After the exposition of the first act, for the successive acts as the curtain rises there is a recapitulation of the story. The widest ranging, though not the longest mnemonic recapitulation of the story occurs, as would be expected, in the final act, where the momentous decisions are made that eventually lead to the play's resolution.

Torres Naharro, like Lope de Vega after him, catered in different ways to different audiences. Lope de Vega considered his theater-going public as a *senado* ("senate") or *jurado* ("jury") that passes judgment on his plays. Torres Naharro annexed his audience to the company of performers. He used the term *compañia* ("company") to refer both to his group of players which presents the drama, and to the audience which sits before it in judgment. In the denouement of the last act when Policiano is reluctant to unfold his story before others and wishes to talk privately with his brother Floristán, the latter reminds him that it would be discourteous and unfair not to let the "company" in on the secret details of his story: "Cata qu'esta compañia/ te son deuotos sin arte,/ y dexar de darles parte/ paresce descortesía" ("See here that this company is devoted to you without reservations, and to leave them out would seem discourteous") (II, 76, 325–28).

The audience-awareness and play-audience relationship that Torres Naharro learned from the classics continues on an unabated scale as the dramatist anticipates typical endings of the baroque drama when Teodoro terminates the last act by turning to the public and speaking in the manner of the concluding remarks of a play by Lope de Vega or Calderón: "Vos omnes iter tenete./ Reliqua mentea prescient:/ hac intus nuptie fient./ Plaudite iam et valete" ("You all have a journey [to make]; minds foresee what remains: weddings happen in this way at home. Applaud now and good-bye") (II, 79, 421–24).

VI *The Cast*

The *Seraphina* is performed by nine characters which, according to Torres Naharro's preceptive limits for a good play, is well within the acceptable number of six to twelve characters in a play. Among the primary characters the following stand out with their identifying features: Seraphina is foxy, shrewd, and vigorous, not quite the seraphim her name would suggest her to be. This may well imply that her name is intended to have ironic connotations. She is a self-centered individual who jostles others to gain her ends. Orphea, the other woman, awakens sympathy with the devoted love she has for her unwilling lover. This Roman girl is a delicate clinging vine, full of self-pity—a victim of circumstances. At the point of mortal danger she is resigned to her fate, offering no violent defense, but stoically pleading for remembrance of her tomb.

Floristán, deriving his name from a king of Sardinia in *Amadís of Gaul*, is a baffled and baffling courtly lover. His courtly love is exaggerated like that of Calisto in *La Celestina*. If taken seriously, he is an abominable character—selfish, weak, irrational, self-deceptive, and ignorantly cruel. Taken lightly, his tragic flaws turn into redeeming, harmless comic attributes. Lenicio, like Boreas of the *Ymenea*, is one of the prototypes of the comic figure, the *gracioso*. Displaying a versatile personality, he is the catalyst, the dynamic comic force behind the play. Educated alongside his master whom he served while the latter attended a university, he combines wit with satire, devotion with cynicism, and love with cowardice. As interpreter of servant life in Valencia, he represents many aspirations of the servant class of the sixteenth century vis-à-vis their masters, holding to the view that only those who use their hands deserve to eat (II, 67 21–22). Despite their careful, deferential treatment, there remained a collision of intentions between the masters and the servants, and the servants still did not enjoy the freedom of action, economic and cultural, that they longed for as human beings.

VII   *Ideas*

Along with the objective to entertain, the author strives for an ancillary didactic expression of personal prudence. Displaying an ironically tyrannical posture toward woman, he champions free will and self-determination in choosing lifelong partners. Torres Naharro's depiction of dissident man's struggle against silently harmonious nature constitutes a cynical commentary on the meaning of life. With discretion, man can moderate his nonconformity with the laws of nature and thus strike a course of action that leads to a more fulfilling life characterized by the Golden Mean. In sum, the play tends toward good organization with its prefigurations and recapitulations and a suspenseful plot with colliding interests providing an interesting conflict based on the eternal love triangle. At the beginning of the play, granted, the characters come and go without sufficient warning, but this is most likely a deliberate comic methodology for unexpected, coincidental meetings. Later the dramatist modifies his farcical stance and works toward situation comedy. As he edges away from farce, he prepares better for his characters' entrances on stage. One may even marvel at the play's technical excellence. Nearing the conclusion of the play, Torres Naharro himself approves of what he considers to be his adroit handling of the story's resolution. After Policiano reveals, to the audience's relief, that he has saved his love solely for Orphea, Floristán asks Seraphina:

> Qué os paresce a uso, señora,
> d'una suerte tan bendita?
> SERAPHINA: Que ne sent gloria infinita.
> LENICIO: Nunca vi mayor ventura.
> FLORISTÁN: Ni se verá en escriptura
>   por manos de hombres escripta.

> What do you think of that, ma'am,
> of such a blessed fate?
> SERAPHINA: I feel infinite glory.
> LENICIO: I've never seen better luck.
> FLORISTÁN: Nor will a better one be seen in writings
>   written by the hand of man.

> (II, 78, 387–92)

Torres Naharro seemingly is content at this point with his own inventiveness, and does not hesitate to communicate this impression confidently to his public.

After the homage to Spanish traditional semireligious theater paid by his *Diálogo* and the *Addición*, with the *Seraphina* Torres Naharro sets out in a radically new direction for the Spanish stage. There now begin to appear trends that later find permanence in his work. Henceforth he embarks on a theatrical formula that is dramatically revised from any seen before in the Spanish theater. In its unfolding, the play-audience relationship is strengthened with the new technique of recapitulation, plus a seriocomic formula, forging the mold for the cape and sword plays and their ubiquitous *gracioso*.

Thematic material that will dominate his theater and many of the productions of the Golden Age, namely, love, is intermingled with corrective social awareness. Torres Naharro has not yet discovered in the *Seraphina* the exploitable ramifications of the honor theme. At this early stage, it has not yet taken hold of his imagination. The only mention of the honor theme is an unimaginative condescending one in which it is the comic character who shows concern with it. This honor is economically rather than socially motivated. Lenicio's servile honor precludes a man from serving two masters simultaneously. After this play, two others must elapse before honor becomes a propelling force in the playwright's work. Later we will see how Torres Naharro constructs a basic aesthetic formula in the revolutionary process of ideas and art for the Spanish *comedia*.

CHAPTER 5

Comedia Soldadesca

A FTER having explored briefly the field of what he termed the *comedia a fantasia*, Torres Naharro turned his creative genius next to the seamier sides of life. In his first attempt at the *comedia a noticia* ("documentary play"), the playwright produced *Comedia Soldadesca* (*The Military Comedy*, 1510). In this play he assailed the uncomfortable depths of nefarious schemes and inglorious transactions among disreputable individuals seeking an agitated haven of welfare in the military services.

I *Synopsis*

The introit is spoken by an anonymous shepherd who, following the earlier pattern set by the *Seraphina*, expresses himself in the Sayagués dialect. Surprised by the number of people he sees before him, he guesses that all of those present are educated and unabashedly presumes they are no doubt presumptuous. This notwithstanding, he maintains that they are ignorant of the simple rustic tasks in which he is an expert. He ridicules the spectators' education by asking foolish questions, and degrades the audience by noting that they came to listen to *este villano* ("this rustic") (II, 142, 39). Philosophizing that contentment is the greatest wealth, he proceeds to ask a rhetorical question, "who sleeps more satisfied, I at night in a hayloft, or the pope in his opulent bed?" (II, 142, 57–59). The poor peasant enjoys his meal of garlic and bread more than the pope who, with his dinner of pheasants, barely touches his food, while the rustic would lick his hands with gusto after his victuals. He summarizes his entire attitude, that of a deprived man who is thrust into the midst of a luxious court: "Yo, villano, / biuo como christiano,/ por aquestas manos más./ Vos, señores,/ biuìs con muchos dolores/ y sois ricos de más penas,/ y coméis de los sudores,/ de pobres manos agenas" ("I a rustic, live longer and healthier and

53

happy every day, and I live like a Christian, by the work of my hands. You, lords, live with many griefs, and are wealthier of pains, and you eat from the sweat of other's poor hands") (II, 143, 75–84).

But upon this daring criticism directed at the noble and the powerful in the audience, the peasant begs their pardon, claiming that he felt obliged to say these things to them because another such opportunity will not present itself to him in the next decade. His apology is prompted by the fact that after all, his intention in coming was to give them joy, not sobering criticism. The narrator of the preface then turns his attention to the play itself and provides a succinct summary of the plot. Our version, somewhat amplified beyond the rustic's statement, is as follows.

Act 1 begins with the words "¡Reniego del rey Ramiro!" ("I curse King Ramiro") as Guzmán, a recruiter, swears that the times are unbearable in Rome. People who glance at others on the street are jailed because there is constant fear of personal assaults and robberies. Guzmán further complains of the wretched state of the world. For him war and turmoil would be an improvement; he is well paid only during periods of conflict. He recalls when young men could turn to the church for their livelihood and become priests, if they could not enter military service. But the benefices have disappeared, and the clergy, like the soldiers, are in a miserable discontented state, with many abandoning the church to seek an improved life elsewhere.

In time of war the soldier receives good compensation and can live well, being provided food and quarters by the peasants. Guzmán laments the passing of Pope Alexander (Rodrigo Borgia), who was good to the soldiers, as well as the death of his son, Duke Valentino (Cesare Borgia, d. 1507?), whom Guzmán used to accompany on inspections, and from whom he received twenty monthly ducats.

A captain appears without previous warning, informing Guzmán that the pope has asked him to raise an army of five hundred men. If the needed recruits are mustered, he promises that Guzmán will be his lieutenant and Manrique his ensign. The captain claims no interest in money, but this remark serves to reveal the covert desire for private gain. Guzmán feels he fits the captain's plans and claims to have fought in several battles including Garellano, Chirinola Bugía, and Tripoli (1510). For his valor in battle, Guzmán tells the captain that he was recognized by the Gran Capitán himself.

Guzmán is then charged with seeking a drummer who would announce the proclamation for recruitment. The captain ponders for a moment and confides to Tristán, an aide, that he understands Guzmán and his types, the soldiers who are, "bravosos,/ muy peynados,/ presumiendo de esforçados/ y siruiendo por antojos" ("boastful, very sleek, presumptuous in their valor, and serving in self interest") (II, 152, 199–202). As he talks with Tristán, he reveals his designs brazenly to further his own interests and to improve his financial condition quickly, inasmuch as papal wars do not last long. He sends Tristán for idle men to perpetrate a fraud on the pope by lining up for pay several times. When Guzmán returns with a drummer who requests ten ducats, a haggle over wages ensues, and the drummer finally agrees on a somewhat lower, indefinite sum and goes out to fulfill his contract.

Act 2 opens with a crowd gathered around the drummer who announces the proclamation for recruitment. Standing by, Mendoça engages him in repartee, and agrees that it is easy to gyp the Spanish simple foot soldier. Mendoça departs seeking the captain and announces that two prospective recruits are coming, Juan Goçález and Pero Pardo. Their conversation with the drummer reveals that three years ago in Spain Juan's wife had thrown him out of the house, so off he went to war in Granada. He has children and must seek the family's daily bread away from home. A begging friar who joins them is told by the drummer that a soldier's life these days is much better than that of a monk, as evidenced by the many friars joining the military ranks. Easily convinced, the friar decides to become a soldier, removing his habit and exchanging it for drink at the nearest tavern.

In act 3 the captain announces that if necessary, he will even rob altars in order to pay his men. Manrique, Mendoça, and the captain argue until finally the latter reconciles them. The drummer reappears announcing that some recruits went to the captain's house. He is responsible for gaining three recruits and speaks of the friar becoming the soldier renamed Liaño. The new *bisoños* ("gimmes"), Juan Goçález, Pero Pardo, and Liaño, are sent to be quartered with Italian peasants where the language barrier forces them into a farcical verbal exchange over demands for food. The Italian peasants decide to send the Spanish mountain boys back to their hills with a beating.

In act 4 Guzmán schemes with Mendoça to pilfer a dozen salaries from the captain. With a padded payroll they plan to go to a big city with a cart full of compliant women. Mendoça surprisingly advises against amassing wealth, because it corrupts the mind and body alike, but along with the others, seeks to do precisely what he criticizes. Juan Goçález joins Guzmán and Mendoça, asking advice about polishing a breastplate which he has been issued. Guzmán and Mendoça plan a joke on Juan, advising him to shine the armor with soap.

Act 5 begins with Juan cleaning the breastplate when his friend, Pero Pardo, enters, pursued by Cola and Joan Francesco, Italians who vow to kill the Spanish soldiers. Cola confronts the captain and states his case against the pilfering recruits. The captain soothes him, promising to pay for whatever his soldiers would take. This turns into a diplomatic feat, when the Italians themselves enlist in his company. Confidently, the captain then details his plan to Guzmán to make fifty percent profit on the sale of equipment to his soldiers. In addition to that, they will also have to pay him for flag, haircuts, a chaplain, and a quartermaster. After this is decided, it is time to fall in and to proceed with the service training. The play ends in a *villancico* sung by four trios, as they march off in military fashion.

II   *Analysis*

This *comedia a noticia*–individualized history on a personalized level–describes an army corps in the making. What was composed primarily to create laughter for the spectators in the sixteenth century, has become today a historical document, depicting aspects of the period's military life.

Since the introit speaker makes references to those in the audience who are still drinking, the play was probably presented after a banquet in a cardinal's palatial home or in the palace of some other prince. Leandro Fernández de Moratín in his critical discussion of the play says, "This play, merely episodic, holds no special interest, nor should one seek a moral lesson in it, an idea which the author did not harbor; he tried solely to make an exact picture of the corrupt customs of a dissolute soldiery, and he was able to do this with facility and comic levity."[1] With more appreciation, M. Menéndez y Pelayo wrote, "This play is not only amusing for its activity and comic levity, but also presents the interest of being the oldest dramatic picture of customs and military excesses, preceding by three centuries Schiller's admirable scenes in *The Camp of Wallenstein*, and likewise preceding Duque de Rivas' scenes in *Don Alvaro*."[2]

More recent critics, such as Gillet and Green, have warmed up considerably to the exquisitely turned dramatic concepts of Torres Naharro. Green observes, "The play is an exposure of rascality, but its perfect objectivity does not imply moral indifference. Certainly not in the angry man who was moved by the corruption of Rome to write the *Sátyra* (Satire) and *Capítulo* III (Chapter III). For Torres Naharro the *Soldadesca* was obviously a heavensent opportunity to relieve his pent-up indignation, . . . when would he ever again have such an opportunity?" (IV, 509). Green agrees with Moratín and Menéndez y Pelayo, however, on the significant value of the play as the oldest picture of customs and military outrages composed in the Spanish language. The drama deals with three types of Spanish soldiers. One is the *plático*, the experienced soldier who can fend for himself, another is known as *bisoño* (Italian *bisogno*, "I need"), a somewhat backward type, in need of help to survive, while the third is a "Guzmán," a synonym for a cowardly, boasting soldier, a literary favorite of the Renaissance and the Spanish Golden Age.

The *Comedia Soldadesca* was written for a particular, educated, bilingual audience consisting of the Spaniards earning their livelihood in Italy. The language of the play reflects the polyglot audience: it is a mixture of standard Spanish, Sayagués, and Italian. The rascally captain speaks both in Italian and Spanish, for his company is made up of nationals of both countries. The Italian vocabulary used in the play is not the standard Italian of Tuscany, however, but a dialect evoking the farming area around Rome. The language barrier between the monolingual Italian peasants and Spanish soldiers gives rise to a great deal of the humor. To contrive effective comic episodes, Torres Naharro makes clever use not only of linguistic elements that contain ambiguity, but also of nonstandard speech. Dramatic irony plays an important role in these situations, where the audience knows something that the characters on stage do not.

The scene of the play is the Eternal City of Rome. The dramatic piece could have been originally presented either in Naples or in Rome with their sizable colonies of Spaniards. The date of the play would appear to be 1510, judging by the mention of the latest battles that Guzmán boasts of having participated in, including the

one at Tripoli fought in that very year. A more significant battle of
Ravenna fought in 1512 is not mentioned, implying that the play was
composed before that battle occurred. There are perhaps some au-
tobiographical statements in the play. Torres Naharro possibly pro-
jected some of his beliefs into the Guzmán type,[3] having presumably spent some time in military service in Italy while harboring
thoughts of becoming a cleric as did Guzmán. From the contents, it
is deducible that Torres Naharro was probably a soldier under Gonzalo de Córdoba and Cesare Borgia. If we go so far as to equate
Guzmán with the playwright, then it would seem that Torres
Naharro may have been a soldier as early as 1503 at the battle of
Chirinola.

There is no plot as such in this work, in the same way that life
usually has no artistically designed plot either. The author offers
instead a series of vignettes, showing attempts to raise five hundred
soldiers in sixteenth-century Italy. In the absence of a plot there is
no requirement for substantial prefiguration nor recapitulation. The
play is written in *coplas de pie quebrado* of eight and four syllable
lines with ten lines to a stanza having the rhyme *a a b a b c c d c d*.
Artistically the play exhibits good dramatic concepts, with traces of
prefiguration and recapitulation, but no confidant-comic figure, nor
any approach to the themes of love and honor.

The drama begins wih order and progresses to disorder, with
minimal order being restored in the final lines. The closing song
speaks of cranes that fly above in formation, thus mirroring the
soldiers' orderly march off the stage. Seemingly irrelevant to the
play, the strophes of the *villancico* ironically express the underlying
difficulties of the vignettes as well as their emotional significance:
"Las grullas en su bolar/ por orden las vemos yr;/ los pueblos para
durar/ por orden se an de rregir;/ . . . Bien es las damas seruir/ y a
cada qual en su grado,/ y penar hasta morir/ en lugar bien
empleado" ("The cranes in their flight, are seen to go in order, and
peoples in order to survive must be governed by order; . . . It is
good to serve ladies, and each one according to her rank, and pine
till death, in a well employed place") (II, 186, 198–201, 205–8).

This play follows Torres Naharro's precepts regarding the number
of *dramatis personae* with enough roles to constitute four trios on
stage at the end, but only ten of the twelve characters speak. Since
his optimum number ranges between six and twelve, this play's
number of characters would be at the upper end of the spectrum.

The charactonyms emanate from ordinary people rather than classical inspiration. This nomenclature is a departure from the dramatist's normal practice in other plays like the *Seraphina, Ymenea,* and the *Calamita.* Unique also is the fact that the dramatist expresses his concern for its organization, very much in the fashion of Gil Vicente's early attempts at playwriting. Torres Naharro is not sure of the play's contents, whether or not they are a proper compilation of events (II, 144, 107). There is no cohesive dramatic event, no one compelling character to unify it. It is a play of sequential action rather than of character, although Guzmán and the captain are impressive as unscrupulous swindlers; the Italian peasants in their hesitant, trembling ways are memorable for their spirit in standing up to the truculent Spanish soldiers in defense of their homes.

Torres Naharro recognizes textually that art is not invention that caters to the obsession of novelty, but the perfection of recognized eternal patterns. The dramatist skillfully blends old formulas with his innovations. Despite his superior skill, he may have been overly rushed to produce this play, as had been Gil Vicente with some of his, but unlike the latter, Torres Naharro specified no excuses, merely asked pardon for the play's faults and for its lack of polish.

The sources for the play are several, some of them are literary, while others would seem to be the actual experiences of army life and of the soldiers that Torres Naharro himself probably knew. Addressing himself to the question of sources, Green writes that "this is the first fullfledged appearance of the military in Spanish literature. The soldier type vaguely emerges from the *caballero* of the thirteenth-century, *Disputa de Elena y María,* of French origin. In Lucas Fernández's *Farsa o quasi comedia de [Prabos y el] Soldado* (probably earlier than the *Soldadesca* which we have tentatively dated 1510) the soldier is still close to the knight of the pastourelle, but the rustic's opinion of him is brutally realistic" (IV, 506). Guzmán's early complaint of the bad condition of the world can be likened to the plaints of the characters of Lucas Fernández in the opening lines of his plays. Such diatribes in Lucas Fernández, however, are not attuned to the socioeconomic times, but are vented against the inclemency of the weather or the harsh cruelties of love. The comic, almost farcical scene between the soldier and the Italian rustics, Juan Goçález and Cola, resembles the scene of the soldier and the rustic Pascual in Lucas Fernández's aforementioned

Farsa o quasi comedia.[4] Fernández's play is dated between 1497
and 1499, so Torres Naharro may have seen it performed before he
left Spain for Italy, or may even have helped to present it in Spain,
perhaps taking a manuscript of it to Italy for presentation there.

III   Social Consciousness and Social Protest

During the first decade of the sixteenth century both Italy and
Spain were struggling through extremely difficult economic times.
Harvests were meager and enormous crop failures were blamed on
droughts and inclement weather; prices of staple foods soared; jobs
were scarce and both animals and humans died of starvation. Predictably, under these conditions voices of protest were heard. Torres Naharro's play exhibits a considerable amount of social con-
sciousness in its protrayal of military life. The soldier's lot that he
presents reeks with corruption and dishonesty. In act 4, the clever
underling officers, Guzmán and Mendoça, after getting their pay,
plan to run off with women. In act 5 Guzmán and his captain plan to
sell the soldier's equipment at a fifty percent markup to the recruits.
On payday men will be hired to stand in line to collect double pay
from the pope. The victim of most of the subterfuge is the plain
simple soldier for whom Torres Naharro paradoxically shows little
sympathy.

In presenting an everyday sketch of the peculiar complexities of
army life of Spaniards in Italy, Torres Naharro reveals the officers
receive twenty to thirty ducats a month, while other soldiers receive
only half that amount. A drummer who wants ten ducats for his
recruiting services has to settle for much less. Soldiers are woefully
underpaid and as is customary in wartime they take refuge in
people's homes and live off the particular family's food supplies.

Like the soldiers, the clergy are experiencing hard times and have
become discontented; they too form a dissatisfied sector of society.
Some of their number, the drama shows, are abandoning the church
with hopes of earning a living in another portion of the economy.
The stability of the church has been undermined, its profession
quickly abandoned for the questionable rewards of a military life (II,
160). The world lamentably no longer needs friars. They are all too
easy to come by: a man can become a cleric simply by buying a used
habit. Attired with it, he can thus give mass, or beg for money to
support himself in the name of holy religion. The quick and easy
change from the cleric's habit to another life is also expressed by
Encina in his play, *Égloga de Cristino y Febea* (1497?), in which

Cristino throws away the religious garb for mundane love when his friend Justino advises him: "Deja los hábitos ende,/ Dalos por Dios, o los vende,/ No los cures de llevar" ("Let the habit be; give it away or sell it; don't think of wearing it").[5] Religious relics and objects are treated with careless abandon. The captain swears to pay his soldiers, even if he has to rob from the altars of the churches of Rome (II, 92). The irony is that when such sacrilegious thievery is done, it is exercised solely for personal, rather than for society's profit.

All the characters attempt to deceive each other in one way or another. Guzmán pretends to be a gentleman, but he is not. He wants to swindle his boss, the captain, whose selfish interests likewise motivate all his actions. The picaresque captain, the friar, the rest of the soldiers, even the Italian peasants, all want to take advantage of others. Torres Naharro's portrayal of conditions in Italy shows that robberies on the streets of Rome were frequent. Looking at passersby might be an indication of a planned robbery in the offing. At night people walked down the center of the bleak streets rather than along their shadowy sides, where danger lurked. The same insecure conditions prevailed in the Spain of Fernando de Rojas. The bawd protagonist of *La Celestina* (1500, according to Vindel)[6] was sure to walk down the middle of the streets at night to keep out of harm's way, drawing away from the shadows of doorways, garden walls, and gates where marauders were likely to be huddled in hiding.

Anticlerical sentiment of the same nature that permeated the entire period preceding Luther's Reformation is visible in Torres Naharro's work. Despite this, he is not antireligious. Even his captain, the foresworn altar robber, uses reverential terms such as "Dios os guarde" ("God keep you") (II, 96) in his daily greetings. Much later, the Council of Trent (1545–1563) attempted to correct the flagrant abuses of church privileges that led Linaño of Torres Naharro and Cristino of Encina to reject the corruption of the religious orders. This vignette of the soldier's life abounds in social protest and criticism from the very introit, with a scathing attack on the rich, vis-á-vis the poor, but also presents the other side of the coin as the author demonstrates the meanness, vileness, and corruption that the poor put into practice against each other as well.

The implicit and explicit social clash is aired in the introit as the shepherd speaks to the cardinals, bishops, and other dignitaries of the audience, all of whom are accustomed to dressing lavishly. The traditionally impoverished rustic, who feels out of place before the distinguished personages, flaunts their wealth before them but feels compelled to apologize for his remarks. Torres Naharro felt strongly for the oppressed but also realized that his primary obligation was to nourish the comic spirit. He felt the need to make the risible deliberately clear in a time of economic distress and social chaos. The times were unpredictable, and Torres Naharro holds a bitterly comic vision that was disenchanted by a society that could trivialize his art and talent. Outraged for the moment, in this indignant introit the long stifled rage of Torres Naharro erupts, only to be subdued before the vignettes of the play which produce the ironically warm, hilarious scenes of the poor soldiers and their commandants concentrating on attempts to raise sustenance from equally poor peasants and destitute vagrants.

The author is able to make his critical charges against both the church and its army, because he speaks from behind the immunizing mask of comedy, attenuating his words when he speaks them through the guise of the rustic prologuist; he thus can maintain that it is not he who loosens the controversial slings of criticism, but rather the ignorant shepherd, whose audacity and naiveté are made more easily pardonable by virtue of his innocuous position in the social order. Even in the medieval tyrant's court the jester was immune from punishment for his satire of the ruler.

Moratín lamented that there is no moral in the play, but clearly, one is readily aware that the playwright's indignation shows in his condemnation of greed and dishonesty in both the upper and the lower strata of society. Eventually the unsavory aspects not only of military but also of urban life cried for reform, and the playwright chose to serve as one of the voices articulating the demands that were fermenting in the inarticulate masses.

The social protest evoked by Torres Naharro in 1510 is of the same type that had polarized society in the Greek and Roman classics, in the Bible, as well as in many other socially conscious works of literature. It is the charge of the "have nots" against the "haves" throughout man's existence. From this viewpoint the *Comedia Soldadesca* is a drama of radical, combined with Christian, inspiration, decrying injustices inherent in human systems. By speaking out on social issues Torres Naharro contributed a sense of hope and fair play to his audience, recognizing man's need to enjoy some measure of success and to experience some sense of fulfillment.

CHAPTER 6

Comedia Trophea

RELATED to the documentary play is the festive play of occasion described also as a pageant, a departure from Torres Naharro's two-fold path of dramaturgy which he was in the process of crystal-lizing. This pageant provides a respite during which the author is consolidating his resources of reality and fantasy. In the *Comedia Trophea (Triumphant Comedy*, 1514), he retreates toward the ritualis-tic pattern of his earliest play while striving to maintain the advanc-ing forms and new directions for the expanding cosmos of the theater. It is a patriotic piece, prepared to commemorate a very special na-tional occasion, and as such occupies a middle ground in the author's binary conception of dramatic categories.

I *Synopsis*

The pageant begins with a rustic salutation articulated in Sayagués by the introit speaker. As in the preceding work, the shepherd proclaims his surprise at the sight of so many people: the hall is filled like a church and the only one missing seems to be the priest. The rustic boasts of his knowledge of church rites, telling the audience he expects to be regaled with money, hens, and even a lamb for Easter, to gain weight along with the rest of them. He then recalls an escapade, the rape of a miller's daughter when he was a vineyard keeper. She dies within a month of childbirth, and he sniffles over the sexual deprivation suffered as a consequence. Then he recollects a contest of *pullas* with a companion. He addresses the audience, asking for control of laughter and criticizing spectators for pretending to be learned. He repeats the truism that one should eat to live, and not live to eat, and points out that overindulgence leads to gout.

The shepherd then turns his attention to the king of Portugal, blessing him for his battles against the Moors and for spending his treasures liberally. The poor rustic, along with the king, is an example of generosity, since, poor though he be, he readily shares his own bit of wine and bread with his fellow creatures. After a momentary lapse of memory, he recalls that he came to provide the people with joy and indicates that a five-act play will be presented, whose contents are as follows:

Fama (Fame) initiates act 1 by recounting the virtues of King Manuel I. Unlike tyrants who consume what their own parents and relatives have accumulated, Manuel, a friend of Christians, spends whatever he has in the struggle against the Moorish foe. To the lands he has inherited, he has added others through his own efforts and those of the extraordinary people of Portugal, who follow the shining, eternal name of Viriato, their inspiring captain of bygone days. For the sake of holy wars the king has conquered more lands than Ptholomeo (Ptolemy) described. Ptholomeo appears from hell to answer Fama and to defend the respect that his work merits. To answer Ptholomeo's question about what the king has conquered, Fama recites a plethora of geographical places, calling Manuel the greatest of all kings. Ptholomeo protests that Fama is prejudiced, praising only the great men and neglecting the meek. Fama argues that she gives each his due, and turns her attention to the twenty pagan kings who come to pay homage to King Manuel. Ptholomeo concedes that Fama can give all due glory to all who deserve it, but by the same token she need not belittle his own accomplishment. After all, even though Manuel conquered lands that Ptholomeo did not write about, the king did not conquer all of those places found in Ptholomeo's work.

In the second act two rustics, Juan Tomillo and Caxcoluzio, come to clean the hall and, spying a dais, one gets up to sermonize like a vicar on saint's day. The two insult each other with *pullas*, inveighing all sorts of bad luck: may you become blind, may your flock be stolen, may they send you to Rome and condemn you to eat forever in a *tinelo* ("servants' dining room"). Their *pullas* cease only when the page enters and chastises them for not doing their work. To atone for their laxity he asks both to sing for him. Thus, they sing a duet, but when asked to do another, they turn it into a verbal joke on the page. When Caxcoluzio indicates they would like to witness what ceremony transpires later in the hall, the page replies they can

come if they bring presents for the prince, heir to the Portuguese
throne.

Act 3, principally a spectacle, is recited solely by one character,
the Intérprete (Interpreter). Professing to feel unworthy to speak to
the king, he will say only what has been told to him to interpret. The
Intérprete introduces the heathen monarchs from Monicongo and
Guinea and other exotic lands. One by one in pantomime, as the
Intérprete speaks, the rulers assert their eagerness to serve their
new king, entrusting themselves into his hands, for he is a good,
humane and just man. They request permission to be dismissed,
and with that the monologue of the Intérprete concludes.

After the impressive spectacle of the exotic kings paying homage
to King Manuel, act 4 opens with the comic rustics returning with
their gifts and infusing new life into the play with their humor. They
extol the future deeds of João, the heir prince to the Portuguese
throne, and are joined by two others, Mingo Oveja and Gil Bragado.
A dispute ensues over who can speak the first words to the prince
and his court. Although Caxcoluzio claims the honor, because he is
medio studiante ("half student"), the drawing of lots favors Juan
Tomillo. The latter delivers his gift to a stand-in for the absent
prince, and brings him a fox along with which he pronounces a
moral: the monarch must be astute and watch zealously over his
flock against its enemies. Caxcoluzio follows; introducing himself
with a humorous bit of genealogy, he offers a rooster, in his words
the most genteel of animals, whose gentility should be imitated by
royalty. The rooster is an exemplary animal, because it guards its
fences, and shares its good discoveries with those about him. Caxcoluzio urges the prince to summon the people whenever he, like
the rooster, discovers something to share. Mingo Oveja's gift is a
lamb, with which he exhorts the future king to be like it, "benigno,
manso y vmano" ("kind, gentle, and humane"). Finally, Gil Bragado
makes his offering of an eagle. The royal bird is an example of
altruism. The eagle "es tan liberal,/ . . . que, comiendo al más
sabor,/ suelta las presas suaues/ para que coman las aues/ que lo
están en derredor" ("is so generous, . . . that, eating with the
greatest gusto, it loosens its prey in order that other birds which are
around him may eat of it") (II, 127, 221–26). Gil Bragado entreats
that "príncipes y reyes,/ aprendáis ser liberales" ("princes and kings,
learn to be generous") (II, 127, 231–32). Mingo is loathe to relin-

quish his lamb but is assured of other choice foods—cabbage, bacon, beef, and a hen—for the road, after which the four shepherds led by the page march off together.

Apolo (Apollo) begins act 5 with prognostications regarding the king's son, Prince don João of Portugal. Apolo hands Fama a sheet of verses and she begins to distribute them. Mingo Oveja seeks a copy, and noticing Fama's wings, asks to borrow them. She agrees, giving him advice about how to fly. Prior to takeoff he recites a humorous prayer in macaronic Latin. Fama, smooth with deceit, tells him to stick out his tongue for the takeoff and in a ridiculously pitiful fashion he jumps off an unperilous promontory only to come tumbling to the ground. Fama gloats over his failure, moralizing: "many want to fly, and then take such great falls that they can not get up anymore for the rest of their life" (II, 135–36, 240–43). Mingo Oveja recovers some of his composure, again requests one of the sheets of paper from Fama, and exchanges her wings for it. The sheet contains a eulogy pronounced earlier by Apolo (Apollo) of Prince João, and also a *villancico* which is sung as a finale in honor of the Portuguese royalty by the actors and the audience.

II *Analysis*

During March, 1514, a splendid, colorful procession took place in Rome in which most of the important people of the church's hierarchy and of the European governments participated. Manuel I, "The Fortunate," fourteenth king of Portugal (1469–1521), was sending news of the Portuguese conquests with impressive exotic gifts to the pope. The Portuguese had penetrated to Moluccas (in today's Indonesia), and returned with new fabrics, spices, and unusual animals. In the parade, trained Indian elephants caused a sensation by spraying the multitudes with perfumed water as they approached within sight of the awaiting pope. The Portuguese embassy arrived in Rome on March 12 for an audience with the pope a few days later. The mission's visit lasted from March until June, when finally the Portuguese entourage departed for home. It was during this commemorative period that Torres Naharro presented his work before the state and church dignitaries and their respective constituents. While the pope did not attend this festival play, it is believed that the Portuguese ambassador and his suite did.

Besides a performance of the *Trophea*, we have no other record of additional entertainments during the Portuguese mission, but it can be supposed there were others. The *Comedia Trophea* was composed to celebrate the Portuguese conquests in Africa, the Indian Ocean, and Indonesia. Gillet in discussing the date of composition of the play, assumes it to be after January 3, 1514, when a letter of King Manuel arrived in Rome announcing the greatest Portuguese conquests in Moluccas, Indonesia (IV, 474). Manuel's letter to the Sacred College was written on September 30, 1513. The news of the conquest was probably known before January through travelers to Rome, but the official letter probably started the preparations for the spectacular reception of the Portuguese mission. Perhaps we can place the play's performance prior to Easter, inasmuch as the prologuist asks for payment that could include a lamb *para Pascua* ("for Easter"). Easter fell that year on April 16.[1] The Julian calendar, in effect since the time of Julius Caesar, was nine and one half days ahead of the seasonal changes by 1514, and consequently Julian calendar's April 16 according to our Gregorian calendar would fall on April 25. The performance of the *Trophea* would seem to be specifically between March 21 and April 25 according to the Gregorian calendar.

The work is a *loa*, a dramatic panegyric, a pageant celebrating recent Portuguese victories in Africa, India and Indonesia, a *pièce de circonstance* ("play of occasion") entitled after the event it solemnizes, as the Portuguese discoverers unveiled their trophies.[2] The play's form, that of a spectacle, places it in a special category of its own apart from the *comedias a noticia* and *fantasia* as it reveals new geographical facts in conjunction with the historic event of the great Portuguese embassy to the Vatican. Marcelino Menéndez y Pelayo, judging the play according to tight dramatic standards, considers it one of the less literarily successful ones of Torres Naharro, placing it on a par with Torres Naharro's earliest play, the *Diálogo del nascimiento*.

The focal point of interest in act 3 are the subjugated kings. This act is a great spectacle wherein the foreign kings present themselves in an official ceremony of homage that radiates reverent splendor. The only words of the act are enunciated with solemnity by the Intérprete, supplemented by the grandiose presence of the oriental kings with their brilliant exotic dress, color, and customs. Torres Naharro does not idealize the kings romantically, but treats them with courteous, solemn respect, with dignity and a certain primitive refinement. The spirit of respect for human dignity is all pervasive in Torres Naharro. Bearing this in mind he seems to speak with tongue in cheek when he has the kings express gratitude to their subjugators. They show no hostility to their conquerors, indeed they welcome their new yokes and acknowledge that their misfortune is only the lack of a Christian faith, the remedy for which they anxiously await through baptism. Recalling this sacrament two years later, Torres Naharro incorporates the baptismal parade into *Tinellaria*.

A didactic element shows up effectively in the last act where the rustics present their gifts to the Portuguese prince with their edifying comments. The symbolic gifts tendered in absentia to young Prince João (twelve years old at the time of the performance), emphasize humanistic attributes and Christian virtues.[3] Among the four gifts offered by the rustics, the fox symbolizes astuteness, the rooster gentility and kindness, the eagle generosity, and the lamb Christian humaneness. Like the gifts of the Three Magi, these have their meaning, serving as a trampoline for didactic purposes, and satisfying the ordinary public's desire to hear its rulers reminded to lead exemplary lives.

Menéndez y Pelayo is of the opinion that the tone of the work does not correspond to the importance of the momentous occasion, and he cites Moratín who claimed it was an insipid dialogue, prolix, with irrelevant episodes, inconsistencies, and coarse jests.[4] Granting its shortcomings, a good portion of the show is entertaining. What appears insipid, at that time formed part of good politics. The praises to the Lusitanian nation and tribute to the greatness of its people pleased the Portuguese audience and their sympathizers. Although there are no exceptionally lyrical lines in the work, there are some good verses even in the encomium of Manuel I. Other segments have lively dialogue, and still others are admirable in their presentation of penetrating observations and of stinging satirical power.

There are nine speaking parts in the play among at least twenty-two other characters who come onstage. There are twenty pagan kings who merely appear in their splendid attire onstage, and seemingly say no word in any language; there are also impersonators of Prince João and of his father the king of Portugal, both of whom figure in the silent segment of the cast. It is conceivable that the introit is spoken by Torres Naharro himself and that he may have also alternately taken the roles of the Intérprete and of Caxcoluzio.

III *Structure*

From a structural point of view there is a certain symmetry to the acts. Act 1 and 3 sing praises of the king, and 2 and 4 are comic interludes with shepherds, while act 5 is a mixture, combining comedy and encomium. A little beyond the halfway point of act 2, there comes a song and dance routine and a foreshadowing of act 4, a tying-in with it through the mention of the need to bring gifts for the king in order to be admitted to witness the spectacle to be held in the hall. Except for the final *villancico* the play is composed in versification of the *pie quebrado* with interspersions of *redondillas*.

There is no progression to a climax. If one is to look for a crisis, it may be found when Mingo Oveja falls to the ground after an aborted attempt at flight with Fama's wings. Mingo's attempt illustrates the reckless optimism of man, offering a prophetic glimpse of the remote future when flight for man, even to the moon becomes a reality. Mingo is derided and shamed, from which stems a moral articulated by Fama that one should not try to be what he is not meant to be, and what he does not have in him to become. If one tries to break the mold from which he is made, he is doomed to failure. With this lesson enunciated, the play is ready to draw to a close, and since there is no intrigue, there is no need for a denouement. There is, then, in this theatrical piece alternation between the elements of spectacle, comedy, and didacticism. In the last act, these ingredients combine to bring a vigorous finale to the show as the piece ends with a rousing song and dance.

The names of the characters are allegorical and generic, rather than individualistic. This pertains even to what appear to be individual's names like Caxcoluzio (Shining-head), and Juan Tomillo (John Thyme), both of which suggest humorous types. Mingo Oveja (Mingo Sheep) and Gil Bragado (Gil Breech) are established rustic names. There is little foreshadowing in the show and hardly any recapitulation.

We have only a vague idea of the scenic configuration of the spectacle, as there is no attentive effort to detail it. The stage business that contributed to the success of the show and likewise to its humor is left entirely to the imagination. There is precious little textual information on these points. The text reveals that Juan Tomillo becomes peeved at a backslap of jovial approval that the page

gives to Caxcoluzio, but outside of this there is little insight into the
stage action.[5]

Humor in the play is partly achieved through the staging which is
extratextual, and depends almost exclusively on the director's ingenuity. Slapstick surfaces in Mingo's attempt to fly: he sticks his
tongue out as he comes crashing to the ground. Fama herself rep-
rehensibly initiates the laughter at Mingo's expense. Language
compounds the humor in the show in the form of the Sayagués
dialect which helps to set the jolly tone for the production.[6]
Macaronic Latin, wordplay and satirical comments contribute to the
levity. The incongruity of corrupted Latin is used to burlesque the
Language of the Catholic Mass. Even though foreign languages are
not used as openly here as they are in the *Tinellaria, Soldadesca,*
and the *Seraphina,* Torres Naharro's awareness of foreign languages
is exhibited in the presence of the Intérprete, whose solemn remarks in Castilian attenuate the incomprehensible exotic languages
that might have been uttered on stage by the potentates of act 3.
The exhilarating, effervescent dialogue present in the *Soldadesca,*
Tinellaria, and *Ymenea* is missing in the *Trophea.* Even the humor
is somewhat uneven, being vibrant at times while a bit flat at others.
The verbal scene is sometimes bleak and patronizing, inasmuch as
the show depends chiefly on spectacle.

A particularly dependable device which combines wordplay,
dialect, exaggerations, and other comic resources is the technique
of *echarse pullas* ("to cast insults"). Understandably, the technique
lends itself especially to satire, and the clerical profession was especially susceptible to it. This is seen in a *pulla* uttered by Caxcoluzio
to Juan Tomillo, "tu muger se lleve un fraire" ("May a friar carry off
your wife") (II, 104, 69). In another gibe at the clerical profession,
Caxcoluzio taunts his companion, Juan Tomillo, for being "hijo de tu
tía" ("son of your aunt") (II, 111, 307), in other words, the bastard
son of a local priest. Priests traditionally called their illegitimate
children "nephews" and these called their unwed mothers "aunts"
(III, 352, n. 307).

This unique spectacle play is neither a *comedia a noticia* nor a
comedia a fantasía but a combination of both. From the point of
view of *costumbrismo* ("portrayal of customs") the *Trophea* does not
fit the category of a *noticia* so well as does the *Soldadesca* and the
Tinellaria, and lacks *costumbrismo* as such. The scenes with the
servants may be realistic excerpts from life, but others with

Ptholomeo, Fama, Apolo, and the Intérprete are not. The unreality
of these acts appears to confirm the dramatist's own avoidance at
classifying this show as a *comedia a noticia*. The documentary aspect of the work is its basis in reality. Not a comedy in the usual
sense, but a festival play, primarily a show, it offers a series of
diversions related only by theme. The theme—the glorification of
the exploits of the Portuguese—reflects a specific occasion: "The
Trophea, is not, properly speaking, an imitation of a human action,
but an action pure and simple—a magic action, with a double purpose, to confirm an acquired situation and to produce one yet un-
realized . . ." (IV, 496).[7]

Consequently, in an appraisal of the play, it seems pointless to try
to apply dramatic criteria to pass judgment on the literary merit of
the *Trophea*, since its purpose and form are distinct from the traditionally structured play as understood today. The *Trophea* is a sequence of scenes without temporal, spatial, or plot unity. It is "an
uninspired series of somewhat disjointed scenes some of them interesting enough in their traditions and contemporary implications,
but hardly satisfying to those who look for a play" (IV, 502), a somewhat unpolished, undisciplined form particularly as regards its lack
of lyricism. Yet it doubtless served its purpose, and even today it is
historically interesting. There is no reason, however, for taking
other critics to task for liking or disliking it.

IV   *Sources and Influences*

The sources for the *Trophea* are many. An idea here, a saying
there, a remark elsewhere, a letter, a topic of conversation, a ser-
mon, a political speech, a festive reception, another play, another
song, all this and much more taken from life was material for the
dramatist to use. With regards to literary works there are traces that
lead back through humanistic elements to the classics and to the
Bible. Some of these vestiges are fairly evident, while others are
obscured by popular traditions which defy classification. The basic
inspiration may hark back to a brief play by Sannazaro written for
the nuptials of Costanza d' Ávalos, duchess of Francavila, whom
Torres Naharro mentions in his dedication to the *Propalladia*.
Likewise the figure of Fama had been incorporated by Sannazaro
into another festival play *Trionfo della Fama*, performed in Naples
on March 4, 1492, to celebrate the conquest of Granada by the
Catholic Sovereigns. Folowing Sannazaro's play there appeared a

Latin one composed by Carlo Verardi entitled *Historia Betica*, which commemorated the fall of Granada, and was performed in the Piazza Navona in Rome on April 21, 1492.[8] Another playlet by Sannazaro, *Farsa dell' ambasciatore, del soldano, explicata per lo interprete*, which was presented along with his *Trionfo della Fama* on March 4, 1492, in Naples may have suggested the interpreter as a narrator for *Trophea's* act 3.

The stage prop of the chariot used by Apollo in Torres Naharro's play is similarly used as a triumphal chariot for Fama's appearance in Seraphino dell' Aquila's *Rappresentazione allegorica*. This play was composed by a protegé of Isabella d' Este and performed in Mantua on January 25, 1495. To reinforce the use of the chariot in Torres Naharro's play we can return also to Vicente's *Auto da Fama* in which Fama "is carried off the stage in a triumphal car amid much general rejoicing."[9] Mingo Oveja's intention to fly with Fama's wings is interpreted by Gillet as an effort to burlesque an attempt at flight made by a carpenter aid of Leonardo da Vinci (III, 373, n. 97).

The *Trophea* had influence on some subsequent dramatic efforts, starting with Torres Naharro himself. In the *Comedia Jacinta* he writes "el águila, señor,/ que comiendo al más sabor/ suelta las presas suaues/ para que coman las aves/ que le están en derredor" (II, 335, 188–92). These same lines appear verbatim in the *Trophea* as we have seen in our synopsis of act 4. Beyond this, there are repeated ephemeral reflections of a germ that two years later is to crystallize into the *Comedia Tinellaria*. The similarities are striking. First of all, the locale of both plays is Rome. In the *Trophea* it is the banquet hall of a cardinal's palace, in the *Tinellaria* it is the *tinelo* ("servants' dining room") of the cardinal's residence. The word *tinelo* itself appears significantly in the *Trophea*. Juan Tomillo in his contest of *pullas* with Caxcoluzio hopes that Caxcoluzio will be sent to Rome to do penance, condemned to eat forever in the *tinelo* (II, 105, 110–13). In the *Tinellaria* penance in the *tinelo* becomes a reality when Mingo realizes: "no venimos aquí/ sino a hazer penitencia" ("we came here only to do penance") (II, 228, 148–49). It is clear by the mention of the *despensero* and the *mayordomo* in the *Trophea* that Torres Naharro already harbors the urge to dramatize the corrupted affairs in the servants' quarters (II, 128, 241–48), and this of course he does.

Torres Naharro is perfecting some devices of dramatic comic structure. In the *Trophea* he essays the technique of accusation fended off by a diverting retort or counter accusation. When the page surprises the rustics playing when they are supposed to be working, Caxcoluzio in self-defense blames it all on his friend Juan Tomillo. The latter then reciprocates and points the accusing finger of wrongdoing at Caxcoluzio, provoking a heated discussion (II, 106, 145–54). This is later expanded into a hilarious scene in the *Tinellaria*. When Tudesco is accused of stealing meat at the table by sliding it up his sleeve, he in turn accuses another companion of stealing bread, causing a verbal free-for-all. Another reliable device for humor is giving ridiculous advice to a naive character who is liable to accept it. In the *Trophea*, Fama takes advantage of Mingo Oveja's vulnerable simplicity, while in the *Tinellaria* Godoy and Moñiz inflict bodily discomfiture on Manchado when they advise the simple rustic to have his eyebrows plucked in order to land an ecclesiastic benefice (II, 252, 386–407). To conclude with influences, the idea of the festival play as seen in Torres Naharro's *Trophea* subsequently recurs in other authors' plays of occasion, such as those to honor Charles V, to celebrate the battle of Pavia (1515), the Peace of Cambria (1529), or the birth of Philip II (1527).

V *Play-Audience Relationship*

In this plotless presentation, one aspect stands out among others: the play-audience relationship is particularly close in this unique show. The audience is apprised of events from the beginning of the action and invited to participate in the ostentatious display itself. The gala ceremonial experiences continue from the introit to the very end of the play when the performance concludes involving the spectators in the spirited conclusion. The rustic prologue commences by promising the viewers joy and merriment. At the end of the show, Mingo Oveja turns directly to the audience to ask for applause before he departs (II, 137). The play terminates with a communal singing of a *villancico* in praise of King Manuel. The audience mingles its voices with those of the performers, reading from copies of the song passed out during the play.[10] This procedure of passing out music sheets was not unusual and occurred at other triumphal processions and events where participation of the audience was desired. Precisely this audience involvement leads Charlotte Stern to deduce that the intent of this drama was a ritualistic one rather than illusory: "Psychical distance is minimal and audience participation actively sought."[11] It must be considered in the light of literary history as "essentially community drama" (IV, 493), entertainment that captures and expresses collective, group, or crowd emotions.

After the prefacing interlocutor asks, in the tradition of the medieval minstrels, for compensatory presents from his audience for his services, he reproaches public opulence by suggesting that he wants to become equally fat. When laughter erupts from the spectators, the narrator turns indignantly to the audience asking for quiet (II, 86, 125–26). He further rebuffs the people because they pretend to be learned. Of course this was an exceptional gathering of the elite of the Roman and Portuguese courts. Although the pope may not have been present, many of his court were, including learned cardinals, lawyers, doctors, and artists serving in the papal palace of Leo X (Giovanni de Médici, 1513–1521). There were such illustrious names as Leonardo da Vinci, Michaelangelo, and Raphael Sanzio; these helped to make the papal court one of the most brilliant of Europe during the Renaissance.

The introit performer's relationship with the audience is further cemented through the theme of food. Since some of Torres Naharro's plays may have been produced as entertainment after or even during a meal in a banquet hall, as was the *Tinellaria*, there is frequent mention of food for various purposes. One of these is to provide contrast with rustic food and the food available to the palatial gathering witnessing the play. This contrast has two results, one comic and the other didactic, heightening the social criticism which Torres Naharro often injected into his plays (II, 128, 258).

In order to retain the audience's interest in this play, Torres Naharro used a composite of techniques designed to attract its wavering attention. The shepherd who recites the introduction alerts the public to the part it is expected to play in the ceremonies: all will sing the closing song for which sheets will be handed out. The lines of the song are comforting as they provide an orderly secure feeling of a hopeful future, heartily sung to a familiar tune, *con esta nueva canción* ("with this new song") (II, 219, 23). The overall feeling of the strong presence of the audience itself is one of the unifying forces of the play, giving added meaning to the celebration in acclaiming the Portuguese victories.

We have come to accept the criteria for gauging the difference between ritual and illusion as the varying degrees of audience participation. The Roman stage offered illusion because separation between players and audience was complete. This separation continued in force as long as Latin was taught in the schools, academies, and universities. With the later development and acceptance of liturgical drama, medieval religious plays reinstated the ritual that had been the norm in the primitive Greek theater. The Spanish Golden Age drama again returned to the illusion present in Roman drama. Torres Naharro's *Trophea* is related to medieval pageantry and liturgical ritual as well as to Renaissance illusion, which was revived with the humanistic drama. Thus the dichotomous *Trophea* adheres on the one hand to audience participation, and to its removal on the other, catering to the audience in both categories as ritual and as illusion.

In this play Torres Naharro revealed his inclination to write an epic, but he was unable to do it. Epics are written in an age devoid of heroes, when heroes are sought in remembrances of times past. The Renaissance, the age of Torres Naharro, still had its heroes; riding high in heroic history, it was writing epic history with its deeds; it did not need to sit back and contemplate the greatness of a former heroic era. Rather than dreaming lyrically of a remote heroic past, the Renaissance people forged their own heroic epoch. In this performance of the *Trophea* there emerged a mysterious communal sense of pride and hope in which mythology, religion, allegory, pageantry, and fervent aspirations blended effectively into an exciting, momentarily unforbidden fusion of fantasy and reality.

CHAPTER 7

Comedia Jacinta

T HE dates of *Comedia Jacinta* (*The Hyacinth Comedy*, 1509–1515) are uncertain. Like the *Trophea* it is a play treading on middle ground between the two types of comedy defined by the dramatist in his *Prohemio* (see the preface of this study). Determined to adhere to the formulaic structure he discovered and applied to the fantasy of the *Seraphina*, further explored with the realism of the *Soldadesca*, and confirmed by the pageantry of the *Trophea*, Torres Naharro with this play reconciles the binary forces of the real and the fantastic.

I *Synopsis*

The rustic, entering on stage, is surprised by the number of people and, confused, does not know what he is supposed to tell them. He recalls that in his younger days he knew what to do in situations like these; he used to be in demand for singing performances at weddings. He further remembers how in his youth he would go to the meadow on a Sunday, chase after girls, and watch the many games the other youths would play there. Recovering his poise at last, he recalls his reason for being before the audience: to present a *breve comedieta* ("a brief playlet"). Sketching the main points of the plot, and urging the audience to hear the playlet in silence, he warns that otherwise they will suffer a curse that even the pope will be unable to absolve. Following this introit and a general sketch of the plot to the audience, the play unfolds:

In act 1 Jacinto is a poor valet verging on despair because he has lost his job. Unhappy and restless, traveling alone, he would go to the end of the earth after a good master. He sees that the virtuous are unappreciated, while the immoral are rewarded; the merely glib of tongue are crowned with greater success than are those endowed with exemplary attributes. While he decries masters who prosper

from the sweat of others and condemns the fact that men are
deemed less worthy than beasts, Jacinto yearns to find the ideal master.

The rustic Pagano, sent by his mistress, Divina, stops Jacinto,
professes respect, and assures him of his friendship; Pagano also
assures Jacinto that Divina's powers will be used to his benefit.
Jacinto recounts his miserable luck and his search for a virtuous
master, reiterating his view of a topsy-turvy world, where the bad
receive favors and the good are considered traitors; where the beast
is treated better than a human and the wealthy only enrich others of
their class. Pagano praises the virtues of Divina, who is generous as
an eagle that shares his prey with other birds. (The same lines
appear in the *Trophea* [II, 127, 222–26].) Divina is compared among
other women to Queen Isabella of Castile.

Jacinto realizes from Pagano's remarks that the latter is a learned
individual and inquires about the protocol with which he is to greet
Divina, being told to be prudent like the ant and a flatterer like the
fabled fox. About to go before Divina, they sight another man approaching, talking to himself. Pagano decides to await him and take
him to Divina along with Jacinto, but first he will eavesdrop to hear
what this second wayfarer has to reveal.

At the opening of act 2 Precioso, a squire, enters, lamenting that
whenever he takes a step, the grass dies under his feet. Loyalty to
friends has only rewarded him with enemies. In prosperity he has
friends, but when in need he finds himself deserted. He recognizes
only four good things in life: wine, oil, fish, and a friend. In this life,
truth is lacking while treason is abundant; the days of Pythias and
Damon are gone, yet he persists in seeking a true friend. Pagano
detains Precioso, who objects to being stopped by such a gross
rustic. Pagano threatens to hang him from the battlements if he
refuses to cooperate, which Precioso finds surprising on the royal
highway, and objects to being forced to go before the noble lady.
Only when Jacinto intercedes and urges him to go willingly does
Precioso agree, conjecturing that perhaps now his luck has turned.
A third stranger appears, and Pagano plans to repeat the same approach to detain him, and to lead all three strangers to Divina's
castle.

In act 3 Phenicio, unlike Precioso, expects to meet trouble on
the long road he is traveling. He considers everything in this life to
be transitory, and bemoans the human search for temporal things at

the expense of the eternal. This world is fleeting and no one is happy, neither the rich who live in fear, nor the poor who live in grief. Therefore, finding no contentment in the secular world, Phenicio wants to enter the world of religion. Pagano ends Phenicio's tirade by asking if he has some affliction, or is fleeing from the law? Phenicio doubts that Pagano, ostensibly a poor shepherd, can help him, and wants to continue on his journey despite Pagano's insistence that he stay and dine with Divina that evening. Phenicio feels his patience being sorely tried. Pagano persists, accusing Phenicio of fleeing from the Inquisition. When a fight is about to erupt, Jacinto and Precioso intervene to establish harmony, and Phenicio is convinced to go along with them. Pagano identifies himself to the wayfarers, and sensing that the three strangers find it psychologically difficult to go to Divina's palace, Pagano decides to summon the lady to them.

In act 4 the three wayfarers, temporarily left to themselves, debate whether to continue on their journey or wait to see what happens. Precioso and Jacinto favor accepting the invitation for dinner on the premise that a woman is bound to be kinder than any man. Phenicio joins Precioso and Jacinto in praising the virtues of women: they deserve men's praises rather than vituperations, while their detractors deserve to be stoned to death; men learn virtues from women, and women's only evils are those which men teach them; women help men in their hours of tribulation, and cure their ills; a virtuous woman is a crowning glory for man. In short, there is nothing good where there are no women. Jacinto identifies himself at Phenicio's request, and then the three wayfarers introduce themselves to each other and agree to behave like true brothers. Precioso wonders how it might be if Divina should take a fancy to anyone of them. Pagano returns describing the glowing beauty of Divina, who is approaching them. Although Pagano offers to be the spokesman before Divina, Precioso suggests that Jacinto should assume that role.

Divina appears in act 5, marvels at the beauty of nature, and feels fortunate to see it. Jacinto pays respects to her in the name of his companions, and each reveals his origin. Jacinto is from Germany, Precioso comes from Rome, and Phenicio has traveled from Spain. Rome is described as permeated with greed, decadence, and corruption, where the pope goes on with his vices. The city is full of refugees from the Inquisition in Spain, and Precioso regrets that he is not a full Jew, for otherwise he would not be so indigent. Pagano becomes the center of interest as he speaks of his wide range of knowledge: the liberal arts, medicine, and magical secrets, such as turning water into wine. Through the use of herbs, cat's-eyes, and special ointment he knows how one can transplant himself to anywhere in the world. Divina is exasperated when Pagano states that with a certain herb he can make them all expel air like two hundred thunders. Pagano prolongs his discourteous remarks until Divina slaps him. She then hastens to change the subject to the goals of the three wayfarers: Jacinto goes wherever luck takes him; Precioso is fleeing from his past life of ungrateful friends but has no special goal; and Phenicio complains of the world in general, though he has no particular goal in mind either. They are advised to cease their journeying, for Divina has enough wealth to share with all of them. She takes two of the three strangers for brothers, and the remaining one for her husband, while her messenger, Pagano, will become their patron. All are happy at the conclusion and join in singing a *villancico:* "One land alone, Rome; one Lord, one God alone; and one lady only, you."

II *Analysis*

The mood and direction of the play is established by the introit and the early scenes. Similar to the *Trophea,* this work lacks a closely knit plot. A conflict of sorts occurs when each wayfarer confronts Pagano for the first time and is detained by him, but this is quickly resolved in a series of solutions to minor crises. The events do not build up to one crucial or climactic point, but a semblance of one could coincide with the long awaited entrance of Divina on the scene, for her appearance has been detained up to the very last act.

The endings of the separate acts do not present any provocative situations to augment interest in the ensuing action. The transitional interest of the audience is retained via the anticipated arrival of each new wayfarer. Each is dutifully announced before the closing of an act. One expects, therefore, at the commencement of the following act to see the stranger on the scene and to express himself with an interesting network of personal problems. Hence, the audience is well prepared for the appearances of the strangers and particularly so for the entrance of their benefactress, Divina. Yet her decision to marry one of the wayfarers is rather precipitous. Lacking in motivation, it can be justified chiefly on the basis of a preceding literary tradition that had been propagated in Spain for short plays in which convention tolerated sudden character changes.

As was seen in the synopsis, the play concludes with a marriage, but the words of the text do not make it clear whom Divina takes for a husband. A director of the play can resolve the ambiguity by designating almost anyone of the three wayfarers as her mate. The decision made at the pleasure of the director of the play was originally, of course, Torres Naharro's. The textual ambiguity makes the play adaptable to changing circumstances and preferences. Thus, the choice of Phenicio as the husband from Spain would be appropriate for a presentation at the wedding of Vittoria Colonna in 1509, when she married Fernando de Ávalos (December 27). On the other hand, Jacinto, hailing from Germany, may be acceptable as the counterpart of the German Duke Esteban of the eleventh century who came to help the counts of Tuscany in their battles against the pope and thence founded the house of Este. Precioso, as a third alternative, seeks refuge in religion, and Divina could satisfy his longing if she is interpreted as a symbol of the church. The play ends in a song summarizing the meaning of the play. Its lyrical expression praises the exceptional kind of woman who is its heroine.

The verses of the play are elegantly written with decorum and seriousness of purpose. The language of the play is a mixture of standard Spanish and of dialectal Sayagués. Torres Naharro uses here a combination of the *redondilla* and *cuarteta* in stanzas of twelve lines each. Although the typical meter of the early Spanish playwrights was the *pie quebrado*, utilized by Juan del Encina, Lucas Fernández, and Gil Vicente, Torres Naharro made more sparing use of it, deviating from the typical procedure that his Spanish contemporaries had previously adhered to.

The *Comedia Jacinta* has unity of time, place and action. The time is that which elapses during the actual performance; the scene does not change, and the action is limited to what is reflected in the dialogue among the five characters: the three wayfarers, the lady, and her servant. In the introit of this play Torres Naharro does not point out the five-act structure. As in the *Tinellaria*, he makes no mention of *jornadas*, normally done in his other plays. Although the play is divided into the usual five acts, they are not strongly defined. The author called this work a *comedieta* ("playlet") since it contained only about half the lines (1301) of his other full-length plays.

There is no extravagant exploitation of the comic devices in this

work. Pagano utilizes the Sayagués dialect, but its humor does not
come across consistently. The language here serves as a vehicle with
a serious purpose and does not lend itself to facetious interpretations. Although Torres Naharro can make profitable use of dialect
and the exchange of *pullas*, as well as other devices which belong to
the farcical comedy, these techniques remain undeveloped. While
the dialect is reminiscent of that found in the corpus of the *Jacinta*,
the device remains quietly dormant. Despite his dialectal
background, Pagano is enveloped in seriousness. His learning over-
shadows the otherwise humorous forms of the dialect, and instead
brings out more of the critical social intent of the play. Along with
this, though Pagano is slapped (which could be interpreted as part of
the formula for slapstick), the slap seems to be given and taken in a
grave rather than comic manner. Instead of providing humorous
repercussions, it germinates serious ones. Torres Naharro thus fails
to capitalize at this point on the facetious dialect, or the comedy that
could be derived from the potentially slapstick situations. He certainly was capable of generating comedy, and cleverly did so in the
introit through the vulgar expressions of the rustic; within the play it
was a different matter. He had a vital message to communicate, and
did not want to mitigate it by low comedy which might have de-
tracted from it. The message was one of social discontent and a
concomitant desire to have the wealthy share more of their good
fortune with those who lived in deprivation.

The play is structured around five characters—one less than the
usual dramatic number that Torres Naharro suggests in his *Prohemio* as desirable, counterbalancing the *Tinellaria* in which the
dramatist oversteps his own bounds with a total of twenty-two
characters. Except for the *Diálogo del nascimiento* and the *Addición
del diálogo*, his earliest known plays, each of which has four characters in the cast, the *Jacinta* contains the least number of characters
of his dramatic corpus.

III Structure

The first act consists of two scenes, not indicated by stage directions. The second act is extremely brief, 120 lines, constituting one
scene, the encounter with the second stranger. The third act repeats
the same structure. The fourth is devoted to the conversation between the three wayfarers, while the fifth act revolves around the
presence of Divina. Clearly, Torres Naharro maintains rather artifi-

cial divisions for this play, making most acts coincide with just one scene, none of which are planned toward an exceptional closing curtain. Only the third and the fifth acts have what may be considered effective curtains. At the end of the third division, Pagano leaves the strangers alone and the three reach their decision of whether to ignore Divina's invitation to dinner or to accept it. The fifth act, of necessity, has a ring of finality to it and thereby a good curtain. Even though there is a lack of a unifying sense of acts and of consistently effective curtains between them, there is an offsetting sense of scenic division. Torres Naharro manages this through Pagano, who announces the approach of each new person onstage. The dramatist at times has his characters simply abandon the stage and fresh ones enter it to start a new scene with few or no introductory words. It is the words of departure which provide the clues that alert the audience to the closing of a scene and the initiation of a new one.

Upon reaching the third *jornada* the rustic dialect with which Pagano had been expressing himself and which he used in the introit has nearly disappeared from his speech. This happens despite the fact that he claims to be a shepherd. Pagano's dialectal traits once again become noticeable in act 4 as he reverts to using *habra* ("speech"), *prazer* ("pleasure"), *posibre* ("possible"), terms characteristically Sayagués in nature. Act 4 serves in part as a delaying element, building up to the appearance of Divina. The fifth *jornada* begins with her arrival. The transition from act 4 to 5 is accomplished through a satisfying obligatory scene. The audience has been told so much of Divina and delayed so long in seeing her that it is a relief when she finally appears. Her long-awaited entrance can be devastatingly dramatic. Her divine beauty is accentuated by her speech, as her words express the beauty of a fresh open landscape, which recalls the theme of *locus amoenus* ("pleasant place") (II, 356, 1–12).

The play terminates with a *villancico* praising Rome, which in the text of the play has been paradoxically downgraded, satirized, and maligned, perhaps for good personal reasons from the author's point of view. The song further extols the virtues of Divina and glorifies the Deity. Structure indicates that Torres Naharro is aware of the technique of recapitulation and periodically has each wayfarer reminisce on his sad plight. Each one's hardships are thus well impressed upon the audience. In the last act Divina herself recapitulates her own role. Up to this juncture, Torres Naharro has deliberately kept the audience guessing about the characters' identities and Divina's appearance.

IV   *Occasion to Honor*

Like several of Torres Naharro's dramas this one is also a marriage play. In keeping with the concept of the wedding play, the action appropriately ends in marriage itself. This view is different from that held by Crawford, Gillet, and Green concerning the original intent of the piece. Crawford has originally proposed that the play was produced as part of the celebration of the return of the Este family to Rome for their reconciliation with Pope Leo X in 1514 (III, 601, n. 128; IV, 524). These views are not necessarily contradictory, however. Besides serving as a marriage play, the drama could conceivably also have been performed as part of the celebrations in honor of the Este family. The date, purpose, and place of original presentation of the play are all controversial.

We have some idea of the date of composition, since there is mention in the play of Rodrigo Basurto in the past tense. Use of this tense could suggest that he was already deceased. His death occurred between 1507 and 1508 (III, 630–32). The matter is somewhat complicated by a mention in the present tense of Queen Isabella of Spain as the equal in generosity to Divina (II, 335, 203). But Isabella, the queen, died in 1504, and Torres Naharro did not start writing plays, at least those that have survived from him, until about 1505 (IV,479). Evidently the queen's generosity continues to be thought of in the present tense, whereas Basurto's accomplishments are considered past history. This disparate use of verb tense for past events augments the difficulties of using textual wording as evidence for dating this work.

The date is related to the personage who inspired the character of Divina for the play, but speculation continues as to who may have inspired Divina. The character lends itself to several interpretations, and several distinguished ladies were probably considered divine enough to qualify for the honored role. Two strong candidates are Isabella d' Este and Vittoria Colonna. Isabella belonged to an old Italian family which originated in the eleventh century in Milan and was identified subsequently with the province of Venice, the duchy of Ferrara, and the city of Mantua. The family traveled to Rome on many occasions. Vittoria Colonna (1490–1547), the more plausible candidate as inspiration for the character of Divina, was an exceptional woman of great personal beauty, a poetess whose renown attracted many literary and learned men to her court (Juan de Valdés, Pietro Bembo, Jacopo Sandoleto, Baldassare Castiglione, Gian Matteo Giberti, Lodovico Ariosto, and probably Bartolomé de Torres Naharro). She married Fernando Francisco de Ávalos, and in her late years was a close friend of Michaelangelo, being personally acquainted with kings and popes, including Charles V of the Holy Roman Empire, Pope Julius II, and Leo X.[1]

J.P.W. Crawford was the first to suggest that this brief play was written to honor Isabella d' Este (1474-1539) upon the occasion of her visit to Rome in 1514-1515.[2] Although Isabella d' Este came to Rome on an official visit in 1514-1515 where probably Torres Naharro saw her personally, he probably knew her earlier at Mantua, as did other writers, both Italian and Spanish (IV, 376-77). In the accounts of the house of Este, there is mention of "Bartolomé, the Spaniard," suggesting that Torres Naharro may have been on the Este payroll. This play could thus have been presented several times including in Naples, and witnessed there by Isabella d' Este. Correspondence by Isabella d'Este from Naples on December 8, 1514, to her secretary Benedetto Capilupi could refer to this (or an earlier) play of Torres Naharro. Isabella writes in part: "Heri mattina invitata dal conte di claramonte. . . . Levate che fussimo da tavola, quelle Signore a due a due incominciorono a danzare alla loro usanza, et dopoi anchor homo et donna insieme. Si danzò di duo o tre hore. Finito de danzare, si recitò una certa farsetta [comedieta in Torres Naharro's terms] alla spagnola che hebbe assai dil galante. Durò circa una hora e meza . . . ."[3] Isabella d' Este's important conciliatory visit to Rome was celebrated by festivities lasting four months.

The strongest presumptive evidence argues in favor of considering this wedding play to have been prepared in honor of Vittoria Colonna who was married in Ischia (Naples) in 1509. Aside from the date, whichever one of the two distinguished ladies the play was written to honor, Isabella d' Este or more plausibly Vittoria Colonna, it honors womanhood in general. The drama glorifies women in the same sense as the Virgin Mary was glorified in other periods. Indeed the epithet, Divina, shows some of this religious connection. In his philogyny the author chastises those who speak ill of woman, including the archpriest of Talavera. Jacinto's words constitute not only an eloquent defense of woman but extol her divine virtues, her powers of consolation, and her inborn generous self-sacrificing nature. Gillet concedes that Vittoria Colonna, marchioness of Pescara, is a possible inspiration for Divina, since she was known by this epithet later in life; nevertheless, he goes along with Crawford in favoring Isabella d' Este for the honor (III, 602). Gilman accepts Rome as the setting of the play;[4] however, our interpretation of textual evidence argue that the stage scene of the play is not Rome, and that the play was originally probably not meant to be performed there, but rather on the island of Ischia.

V *Sources*

Of the many sources for the play, some obviously derive from well-known works of literature or history, while others are from little known or inaccessible works. Some sources may redound from oral tradition, or from oral comments by friends, or by people of Torres Naharro's acquaintance. The possibilities for sources are innumerable. One of the recognizable seeds of the play, the news theme, is very old. Equally ancient is the oriental story of the fox, cheese, and crow which is perpetuated in medieval Spanish and seen in the *Libro de buen amor* (*Book of Good Love*, 1330) and repeated by Torres Naharro (II, 337, 257). The coetaneous topical element is reflected in the satire of Rome and in the debate over the perniciousness and the virtues of women. Other biblical seeds are manifest in the comment Jacinto makes that "es corona del varón/ la muger qu'es virtüosa" (II, 352, 1522) ("a virtuous woman is a crown to her husband," Prov. 12:4). The theme of false friends is similarly old (Prov. 19:6, Job 16:20). It reappears in Patronio's story of the half-friend in D. Juan Manuel's *El conde Lucanor* (*The Count Lucanor*, 1335) and in many common proverbs. The influence in Torres Naharro of Jorge Manrique's *Coplas* (*Couplets*) is pervasive, though often somewhat diluted and subdued beneath the surface of the words (II, 343, 36–47).

Vital reflections from *La Celestina*, like the *Coplas* of Jorge Manrique, left a lasting impression on Torres Naharro. He was predisposed to think along parallel lines with Jorge Manrique and Fernando de Rojas. Gilman in his analysis of the *Jacinta* stressed the turbulent plight of the new converts to Christianity in Italy. Persecution infuses the feelings of the characters in the *Jacinta* in the same way that this feeling of persecution lurks in the background throughout *La Celestina*. Gilman writes that "Rojas transformed his

'desesperación' into other terms, Torres Naharro perhaps less profoundly anguished than his predecessor—was able to use dramatic
dialogue to give comprehensible form to his own experience."[5]
Gilman further observes, "Divina, the heroine of Torres Naharro's
curious *Comedia Jacinta* (based on the theme of the news), appears
in a posture representative of the age: *Poníase a la ventana/ muchas
vezes a prazer/ con voluntad y con gana/ de nueuas nueuas saber*"
("Many times with pleasure she would appear at her window with
the will and desire to learn of new news") (II, 327).[6] Additional
parallels or sources can be seen in the *serranas* ("mountain girls") of
Juan Ruiz's *Libro de buen amor*, and in the archpriest of Talavera's
El Corbacho (The Scourge, 1438). Torres Naharro rounded out the
popular news theme by using three types of traditional social com-
plaints: these were directed against masters, false friends, and the
world in general. The sources of this work are no doubt many more
than those we have observed here, for after all, books beget other
books.

Drawing interest chiefly by expressing social ideas, this play
avoids a story line but compensates in the direction of individual
characterization. Divina, the beautiful, enigmatic lady, adored and
deified, becomes more than a mere representation of carnal reality,
an allegorical figure symbolizing at one and the same time woman-
kind, the city of Rome, and the Christian church. Divina is, as
Pagano relates, a *nobre muger* ("noble woman"), and "es la más
merescedora/ que ay de leuante a poniente" ("the most deserving
woman there is from east to west") (II, 340, 83, 89–90). She is like a
ray of sunshine that dispels all sadness and radiates joy, pleasure,
virtue, love, nobility, charity, and courtesy.

The male characters are classified in this way: Jacinto is German,
and an old Christian; Precioso is a Roman convert; Phenico is a
wandering Jew; Pagano is a Moslem. They are variously termed as
gentil hombre ("gentleman"), *galán* ("young man"), *hombre de pro*
("man of means"), and *escudero* ("squire").[7] Precioso travels en-
shrouded in the darkest clouds. His thoughts seem to be inspired
most by the theme of friendship as it is reflected in Rojas' *La Celestina* and Petrarch's *De remediis*. His gloom disappears, like that of
his companions, when they fall within Divina's radiance. Phenicio,
more vehement than Precioso, is sick of the entire world, yet not so
despairing that he does not want to have life continue. He has an
independent strong will that marks him as the most stubborn of the
three wayfarers.

Jacinto is ostensibly the hero and the one who should get to keep the girl. On this basis, Green and Gillet believe him to be the one chosen as Divina's husband (IV, 523). However, the actual evidence from the text of the play is inconclusive. Granted, the husband could possibly be Jacinto, but it could very well be Phenicio, the Spaniard, the most likely condidate if we interpret Divina as symbolic of the church, whose shelter Phenicio has been seeking for his tortured spirit.

Of the five characters in the play, Pagano is perhaps the most fascinating: knowledgeable but impertinent and unmindful of the feelings of Divina, he is *medio escolar* ("half scholar") and *medio villano* ("half rustic") (II, 259, 115).[8] Divina shrewdly observes that this gross shepherd can compete with any sermonizer. Pagano is the individual who most closely resembles Torres Naharro. He recites the introit (usually identified with the dramatist himself) and ranks himself among the converts who are anticlerical but not antireligious (II, 328, 114).[9] In the end, Pagano acquires satisfaction through the post of patron, and this may very well signify that Torres Naharro achieved favor with the lady represented by the protagonist in becoming the organizer of festivities in her household.

VI *Social Awareness*

Criticism leveled at religious ranks emphasizes that Torres Naharro did not hesitate to criticize the excesses and abuses of dignitaries within the power structure of the Christian church. It is evident, judging by what Phenicio says, that his creator, Torres Naharro, is staunchly anticlerical: "hallaste a tu muger/ en casa de algún abad" ("you found your wife in the house of some abbot") (II, 344, 83–84). He reaches even to the highest Catholic See as he mocks the pope and his Renaissance court: "La corte tiene fatiga,/ y el Papa s'está a sus vicios" ("The court is tired and the Pope's at his vices") (II, 358, 65–66). Through the *Comedia Jacinta* Torres Naharro uncovers the agonizing life of Spanish converts who seek a haven in Italy. Yet, despite the bad things said of Rome in this play, as Gilman has aptly indicated, the city was, on the whole, good because it served as a refuge for those persecuted by the Spanish Inquisition. The final song of the play proclaims grateful praises to the Eternal City.

Although the work is a wedding play, Torres Naharro has injected into it strong expressions of social protest. Times were difficult in Spain, and those who sought relief to their conditions by going abroad to the New World, to Africa, and to other parts of Europe and especially to Italy, at times found themselves entangled in a hopeless state of human affairs. Through much of its text the play touches on the unbearable lot of some of those people. In Jacinto's initial speech we sense the typical tirade of Torres Naharro on this topic; the difficult economic times are reflected also in the *Soldadesca* and in the pages of *La Celestina*, written about a decade earlier. The plight of the unemployed is intolerable, that of those employed as servants is little better. The grumbling against masters appears with insistent frequency in Torres Naharro's theater. Servants in his works, as in *La Celestina*, consider themselves the equals of their masters, and the latter go to great pains to make it appear that they indeed treat them as such. Sometimes they deal with them condescendingly in order to forestall the dangers that stalk in the breasts of their alienated servants.

Torres Naharro held the Christian view that people who are fortunate should share their good fortune with those who are less so. Divina maintains, "quiero ayudaros/ con aquello que podré" ("I want to help you with what I can") (II, 357, 47–48), and altruistically suggests, "partamos quanto yo tengo" ("let's divide all that I have") (II, 364, 279). The Christian doctrine of sharing all that one has is also found in *La Celestina*. In a rather isolated, almost momentary agreeableness and altruistic intent, Celestina promises Sempronio that all she possesses will one day become his (*La Celestina*, I, 197). In another social commentary parallel to that of *Léa Celestina*, Precioso reflects sentiments held by Areúsa, protegée of Celestina, concerning life in servitude. Precioso says, "En Roma los sin señor/ son almas que van en pena" ("In Rome those without lords are like souls in punishment") (II, 358, 73–74), but life with them is worse than death.[10]

In their common dissatisfaction Jacinto, Precioso, and Phenicio may reflect attitudes of the author himself. After a trying period of spiritual depression and pessimism, the author clings to a solution of a dreamlike existence when his characters triumphantly reach a consoling goal at the end of the play. Thus he strikes a preoccupied stance with unemployment, the wretchedness of life, and the widespread corruption in Rome, to which he can offer only the solution of distribution of already accumulated wealth. Prior to the Reformation, economic, political, and religious difficulties seemed to demand radical changes in the affairs and policies laid down by leaders of the day. The church, which had dominated politics, was beginning to cede its preeminence to the rising new nobility. The secular rulers were struggling to supplant the power of the church in the same way that it had supplanted the power of the ancient emperors of Rome. Torres Naharro is symptomatic of the times, reflecting the thinking of a large section of the masses and of portions of the aristocracy together with some of the church hierarchy itself.

The dramatist, a cynic who understood human psychology only too well, willingly empathized with the sincere emotions of others. All was not well with Torres Naharro's world; but despite the sad plight of the characters, the hopeful outlook of the play gave the nineteenth-century critic, Menéndez y Pelayo, the impression that what stood out chiefly in the piece was its Christian hope of satisfactory solution of the problems depicted. Menéndez y Pelayo judged the work's principal merit to be its consoling, optimistic philosophy.[11] The combined force of its idealistic, redeeming outlook and its bold utterances on realistic deplorable human conditions make this play, like the *Soldadesca*, an entertaining and at the same time a significant document of individualized history and social awareness.

CHAPTER 8

Comedia Tinellaria

THE cynical realism of portions of Torres Naharro's preceding plays, especially the *Soldadesca*, is intensified with *Comedia Tinellaria* (*The Mess Hall Comedy*, 1516?), a documentary comedy of manners dealing with a boorish, clownish conglomeration of immigrant nationals in Rome. Torres Naharro expands his formula, adapting it here to a churlish mob-scene situation.

I *Synopsis*

The introit is recited by a modest would-be poet overwhelmed among palatial dignitaries. He announces that this is an unusual play of many tongues (six languages of the seven parts of Spain) such as are used in the typical *tinelo* (a small dining room for servants found in many of the palaces of Rome). The monologuist notes that the bahavior of people in the play is to be laughed at, but such behavior should be castigated in one's home. The play's name is derived from *tinelo* just as Plautus' *Asinaria* is derived from *asino* ("donkey"). Humbly asking pardon for the author's errors and noting that the play will last two hours, he summarily relates its events. No further introduction is needed, says the prologue speaker, since the place and the characters are familiar to all. The audience can continue eating, or for a price the spectators can buy a place plus food, if they have not already done so. Thus, they can enjoy the play while having a meal.

Act 1 opens early in the evening. Barrabás, the *credenciero* ("keeper of the wine") awaits the washerwoman, Lucrecia, whose services he remunerates chiefly through pilfering from his job in the cardinal's residence. Upon her arrival, the two engage in a petty quarrel; she feels neglected by Barrabás, and laments having decided to accept him as a lover. Regretting former more generous lovers, she mourns the departed mistress who treated her well, giving her many valuables from India and Venice. Barrabás tries to assuage Lucrecia with a kiss, but finding that insufficient for her, he goes off to bring her some tidbits from the pantry. Behind his back Lucrecia shows hatred for him. While he seeks to satisfy her whims, she is determined to give herself to another man. Nevertheless, Barrabás, upon a promise to bring her food and drink, manages to arrange to see Lucrecia later that evening.

As Lucrecia exits, Escalco (maitre d'hotel and Barabás' immediate superior) appears and the two comment on Lucrecia's strong sexual drive despite her forty-odd years. Barrabás praises her as being the equal of any four women in bed. He refers to one of his neighbors, a "Celestina," who has reminded him that the older the hen, the better the meal. Escalco confides that he would also like to have a concubine—an abbess or even a prioress would do. They then turn to the task at hand—preparing the family table by summoning the French cook, Metreianes, to instruct him on the food's preparation.

Escalco and Barrabás plot to administer a beating to Metreianes and to Canavario, the wine cellar attendant, who competes with them in the pilfering from the pantry. They gossip about their underlings and plan a private feast. Mathía, a servant from Andalusia, interrupts the two with a summons to eat at the servants' table before the food gets cold. Escalco responds to the call, while Mathía remains with Barrabás to finish setting the table. Barrabás offers to provide Mathía with a woman: Lucrecia will invite them all to eat together that evening. Mathía is delighted, and Escalco returns to urge them to come to eat.

Act 2 begins the next day before noon with anticipation of a meal by the servants. It is soon discovered that wine, their most important item, is missing. A Portuguese servant makes repeated ethnic slurs against the Jews, while Francisco, a Spaniard, feels these are directed at him. The Portuguese argues with the other Spaniards over politics and the military prowess of their respective countries, as each chauvanistically defends his own. A Frenchman and a Basque join in, and Fabio, an Italian servant, and Miguel from Valencia likewise enter the dispute. Everyone seems anxious for a military contest, but Escalco opportunely arrives to quiet things down, just as two gentlemen's gentlemen, Godoy and Moñiz, enter on the scene. Moñiz upbraids his lackey, Francisco, for not attending to him properly. Francisco in turn claims he is underpaid. Moñiz and Godoy decry the inferior quality of food served in the *tinelo* and

Act 5 takes place in late afternoon. Escalco and Mathía discuss how best to obtain rewards from masters. Escalco, like many other Spaniards, came to Italy in hopes of getting a cleric's job, but is unable to find a position. He feels that anyone's good service should be recognized, and duly compensated without the need to beg for it. Escalco feels that the Spanish cardinal should naturally favor Spaniards when he nominates candidates to new positions.

Canavario joins them, bringing wine which they find better to their taste. When they call Barrabás and Metreianes to join them, the deacon appears, but they tell him he comes too late to be admitted to eat. He is criticized, for he has a good income, but will not spend anything to save himself from starvation. If he wants to eat, he can go to a nearby tavern. They observe that he will not spend any money, and instead he comes to take advantage of the food at the *tinelo*. The door to the servants' dining room keeps opening for new people to eat, and those who are permitted to enter have a good time satiating themselves mainly with drink. Confusion increases as they become progressively inebriated. Dusk falls and they light a candle, then pretend to joust while falling to the floor. Despite his stupor, Escalco asks to be pulled up for a dance; all ends in darkness with the turbulent merrymaking of a drunken orgy. Mathía concludes the drama by directing his final moralizing words to the courtly audience to remind it of "these thousand traitors" who damage "your honors."

II   *Analysis*

This is another *comedia a noticia,* a comedy of current events, a long, boisterous *entremés* ("interlude") which is colorful, picturesque, and at intervals hilariously funny.[1] In it Torres Naharro depicts impressionistically what he saw daily with his own eyes probably in the palace of his chief protector, the Cardinal Bernardino López de Carvajal.[2] This realistic drama was probably composed between 1515 and 1516. About two years earlier Torres Naharro's creative mind was already gestating this play. In the *Comedia Trophea,* performed in Rome in 1514, we saw one of Torres Naharro's characters utter a curse at another, that he be sent to Rome and be condemned to eat forever in the *tinelo* (II, 105, 108–12).

Except for the *Jacinta* and the *Diálogo del nascimiento,* the *Tinellaria* has the least number of lines in the prologue, but contains the largest number of personages: twenty-two. It has 2,463 lines of verse of the *pie quebrado* type,[3] a total of verses exceeded only by those of the *Seraphina, Calamita,* and the *Aquilana.* The *Tinellaria* is one of four plays that do not end in a ballad, but the play does contain music and some dancing at its conclusion. As most of the introits, this one announces that the play is a *comedia,* but it does not mention the five-act structure, nor does the prologuist forget momentarily, as in the *Trophea, Aquilana,* and *Seraphina* what he had been sent on stage to do.[4] As in two other plays (*Soldadesca* and *Trophea*), he says he wants to make the audience laugh, and (as in the *Soldadesca*) asks pardon for what the players will say. If the author errs, he claims, it is the product of ignorance and not of maliciousness.

This prologue differs in other respects from the others. It refers to the extraordinary nobility of the audience: "tan alta compañía . . . tan noble gente . . . tanta magestad" ("such high company . . . such noble people . . . such majesty") (II, 190). Its language is more discreet. There is no rustic jargon, and the frequent obscenities and erotic element are likewise missing, as they are also in the introit to the *Soldadesca.* The play was performed for the first time before Pope Leo X, before his cousin and right-hand man, Giulio de' Médici, as well as before the Cardinal Bernardino López de Carvajal, to whom Torres Naharro dedicated the play. The rest of the audience probably included the brilliant papal court, its honored guests, and official retainers of the Carvajal palace. Possibly even Leonardo da Vinci was to be found among the spectators, (he was in the service of Pope Leo X between the years 1512 and 1516, the period during which this work was written and performed). What elicited easy laughter from the first audiences holds the value today of a magnificent historical document as do the *Soldadesca* and *Jacinta.* Even so, the play has certain characteristics of a farce, manifest particularly in the last act when the meal degenerates into a preposterous orgy.

In the structure of the play, there is no apparent plot, subplot, or line of intrigue that need be pursued step by step. Hence, the closest approximation to a recapitulation is a brief sentence to the effect that "no me penséis espantar,/ aunque vengáis en quadrilla/ y en tinelo a brauear/ mientra come la familla" ("don't think you can scare me, even though you come in a gang and to bluster around in the *tinelo* while the family is eating") (II, 231, 256–59). This is in essence the central theme of the play, the noisy turmoil in the *tinelo*, the petty jealousies and rivalries of the servants. Besides the humor arising from the fresh dialogue, laughable incidents can originate in the genius of the director and in the stage business he utilizes. Most, if not all, of the stage action is implicit in the dialogue, with only explicit indications of music. In act 5 of the *Tinellaria* there is for the second time in the play a hint of a song (II, 264). The play ends without a ballad, but with music and a general call to a dance (II, 266). The music provides relief from the rapid fire chatter of conversation, and the dance at the conclusion augments the general merriment, being a dance of revelers in pairs or in weaving chains of four as the actors stagger from the stage, and perhaps lead to the general dance at the conclusion of the banquet performance.

The *Comedia Tinellaria* is the only play in which Torres Naharro indicates performance time, estimated at slightly over two hours. Why the time element is of importance to the author for this play is not clear, but by its mere mention, Torres Naharro shows his concern for the audience by sharing this information with it. The preoccupation with sustenance, the concentration of the action in one place, and the linear chronological development increase the unifying aspects of the comedy. The period of the action covered by the play's episodes seems to be from sunset to sunset, possibly at two different seasons of the year.

Clues from the text seem inconsistent with respect to the season involved. At one point, the time of year suggested is the middle, "Es la mitad del año" ("It's the middle of the year") (II, 196, 3), while at another point late in the play it seems to be the end of the year (II, 261, 219). It would appear, then, that act 1 takes place in the middle of the year, while the last act, rather than being on the following day within a twenty-four-hour period, could be taking place during a cold spell, possibly before Christmas. It is conceivable that the author tried to present the *tinelo's* daily action at separate times of the year.

The first act is believed to take place one hour after sunset; the second opens sometime during the morning; the third act shows the first sitting of the *tinelo* in the afternoon; the fourth depicts the second sitting later in the afternoon; and the last takes place after the afternoon meals are over (either in the summer or winter) when the subalterns of the household congregate for a private repast that continues until dusk. The play's action concentrates on successive mealtimes and is selected from approximately a twenty-four-hour period constituting one typical day in the *tinelo*. If the references to hot and cold weather are accurate ones reflecting the seasons, then the acts can come at any time of the six-month period from June to December, and the meals are simply mealtime vignettes any time of the year without recourse to specific limitations of sequential hours or days.

III *Sources and Influences*

The sources combining to produce a play like this one are manifold and, as for the other plays, not easily discovered. Some inspiration may come from earlier folk stories and from pieces like those of Plautus, where a cook is synonymous with "crook," and wherein the roistering slaves (of the *Stichus*) may suggest the final roisterous scene of the *Tinellaria* (IV, 516). Other inspiration may come from more contemporary works such as *La Celestina*,[5] but in the final analysis, a play that emphasizes current events depends to a considerable degree on personal observation.

Torres Naharro claims that there are few comedies like this one. There may be several reasons for this assertion, but the principal one is that this is the first play in Spanish to show life in the servant quarters of a wealthy palace. Expressing the uniqueness of his work, Torres Naharro is like the author of *La Celestina*.[6] In addition to the reminder of *La Celestina* there is once again an echo of the impressive *Coplas* of Jorge Manrique.[7] We may further see resemblances to the *Auto del repelón* of Juan del Encina, where rustics are duped into becoming "learned" by having their hair pulled. So in the *Tinellaria*, if servants will not take their turn on watch, they will not be allowed to eat for a month, and if again they fail to take their turn, their hair will be pulled, to be bald like a learned man, "lo haremos licenciado" ("we'll make him a master") (II, 236, 424).

Torres Naharro's awareness of *La Celestina* is underscored by his mention of a "Celestina" as one of Barrabás' neighbors (II, 202, 247). The aphoristic expressions sprinkled in the *Tinellaria* are reminiscent of *La Celestina* and likewise of a work that appears later, the *Lazarillo de Tormes* (1554). It is not necessary here to make a detailed comparison of the propensity to use popular sayings in these works. A further parallel appears when Moñiz, with gentlemanly pretensions, like the squire of the third chapter of *Lazarillo de*

Tormes, insists that he never takes off his cap to the Mastro, a colleague in the *tinelo*, without the latter's taking his cap off first. In both *Lazarillo de Tormes* and *Tinellaria* the authors speak resolutely against presumptuousness. Torres Naharro speaks in the *Tinellaria* of "hombres de fantasía" ("men of airs") (II, 260, 171) in much the same way as the author of *Lazarillo de Tormes*, "quisiera yo que no tuuiera tanta presumpción, mas que abaxara vn poco su fantasía con lo mucho que subía su necessidad" ("I should have liked that he not have had so much presumption, but rather that he had lowered his airs a little as his needs climbed higher").[8] Godoy, another squire in the *tinelo*, has a father who, like that of Lazarillo, died in the war.[9]

There is yet another similarity. Torres Naharro has Lucrecia utter a phrase, "Me lauas la cabeça / después de descalabrada" ("You wash my head after breaking it") (II, 199, 148–49), which leads us to Lazarillo's blind master who breaks the wine jug over Lazarillo's face, and then laughingly washes the wounds with the wine that inflicted them.[10] The similarities between the *Lazarillo de Tormes* and the *Tinellaria* are seen here from the point of view of common ideas. Beyond these similarities, Gillet also noticed that Aretino probably also knew the *Tinellaria*, for he presented in his *Cortigiana* (1534) (act 2, scene 6) a dispute on the sharing of a room that resembles the arguments presented by the squire, Osorio, to the Mastro, in the *Tinellaria* (IV, 513, n. 1).

Inasmuch as there is no unified progression of action, the play stands as a *cuadro de costumbres* ("picture of customs"), revealing a phase in the life of the *tinelo*, a microcosm of the melting pot that was Rome in the Renaissance period. Certain specifics reflect the times: mentions of places, people, and things in Rome; the Burgo Viejo, the Campo de Flor, St. Peter's, and the *Judería* (the "Jewish Quarter"); and the unearthed statue that came to be known as Mastre Pasquín, public gossip figure,[11] as well as references to current wars, to politicians, to leaders (the Sophy of Persia), and to architects (Mastro Bramante, the initial engineer of St. Peter's in 1514). There are references to the oriental trade in Lucrecia's recollection of the products her late mistress used to bestow upon her. Trade from India was then being channeled through Venice. Old clothes were bought and sold by Jewish merchants. There are also unfortunate ramifications of anti-Semitism in act 2. Ethnic slurs are articulated by the Portuguese against the Jews. A sizable Jewish colony in Italy at the time was aggrieved by reports of bloody riots in

Lisbon against Jewish inhabitants of the city. The vehemently quar-
relsome nature of the servants exhibits the malaise, discontent, and
subconscious search for escape from the frustrations encountered
among the lower social classes of the day.

The play of current events exposes topics of conversation that
were relevant and very up to date for its audience. As the minor
officials come to the *tinelo* to eat, they carry on their grumblings,
gossip, and jesting conversations. The greedy search for food was a
taxing problem. Apart from the demeaning accusations of food rob-
bing, the third act is a gem of humor, showing the peculiar comrad-
ery in the scullery. The scene of quarreling, of slapstick confusion
and mayhem interlaced with criticism of the servants' troubled life,
and discussions of political questions produced the hilarity of this
comedy. Like Cervantes, Torres Naharro could be extremely adept
at handling group scenes.

In the concluding moments of the performance the uproarious
noise dies down and Mathía turns to the spectators to pronounce his
admonition: "¿ Veis, señores?/ De aquestos ay mil traidores,/ si
queréis poner las mentes,/ que gastan vuestros onores;/ y vosotros,
ignorantes./ Honrra y vida/ vos la mande Dios complida/ con renta
que satisfaga" ("You see, ladies and gentlemen? There are a
thousand traitors like these, if you want to notice, who waste your
honors; and you remain ignorant of this. May God send you a
fulfilling honor and life, with an income that will be satisfying) (II,
266–67, 380–87). It is meant not only for the pope, prelates, and
princes of the church in the audience, but also for their servants,
who uninvited, stand in the doorways, in the side aisles, and in the
shadows of the balconies of the great banquet hall of the palace.

The spirited, merry, rollicking mood ends on this sober note, and
sobriety reigns as an appropriate culmination to a series of views of
the uninhibited, clamoring, tumultuous, parasitic, and sometimes
brutal life in the *tinelo*. The social criticism in this play is not as
explicit as in the *Soldadesca* (also presented before an audience of
the church's hierarchy). Perhaps the only sugar dressing around the
satire of the servants and their masters is the one that surrounds the
many nationalities. No ethnic preference is expressed; the types,
without exception, are ridiculous: the Portuguese, the Sevillian, the
German, the Valencian and the Basque, and the Frenchman, Peti-
ján, (in the role assigned by the dramatist as champion of civilization, perhaps most ridiculous of all). The mitigating circumstance in

this play of Torres Naharro's vigorous condemnation of *tinelo* life is his cosmopolitanism, or more precisely, his human universality. Social criticism no longer focuses on the elite but spreads down to the neglected, the disadvantaged, who exploit their own peers. In this play, as in the *Soldadesca*, although Torres Naharro is the underdog's champion, he is likewise a severe critic.

With so much anticlerical sentiment in this play, it is difficult to visualize the presence of the clergy, including the pope, at the play's performance. Yet as Pagano observes in the *Jacinta*, someone has to tell the truth, and here it is the dramatist who has decided "to tell it like it is." In occasionally unrestrained terms the pope and the cardinal are made aware of what those who serve them are thinking and doing, even when such revelations are not flattering to the audience.

IV *Play-Audience Relationship*

The reminder to the people watching the play that they can purchase a seat and a meal, if they have not already done so, and that they can continue eating as they watch the play, evokes conditions for the play's performance similar to those of present-day "dinner-theaters," where the price of admission includes both a dinner and the performance of a play. As is the practice today, most of the audience probably finished eating by the time the performance began in the banquet hall.

Torres Naharro's devastating satire does not spare even the nuns, when he employs the colloquial terms "prioress" and "abbess" to refer in slang to prostitutes and madams[12]—a shocking feature in a play presented before the pope himself! Yet even more daring seems to be the critical, sarcastic exchange that took place between Godoy, on the one hand, and Manchado, on the other, relating to papal appointments. Poor, naive, and uneducated Manchado had come from Seville to Rome in search of a sinecure. Why? Because "El Papa diz que los da/ a todos quantos los quieren" ("They say the Pope gives them to all who want them") (II, 251, 358–59). Political abuses immersed in the religious structure were widely known and discussed on all levels of the church's organizational spectrum. The church controlled much of the economic and political life of the period and thus was open and subject to hostile criticism at every turn, its sanctified ambience having become too mingled with mundane political operations for it to remain exempt from justified censure.

Despite the brawling, naturalistic disputes among the servants, the various acts carry appreciable profound philosophical commentary. The relatively frequent use of proverbs lends a penetrating, universal tinge of wisdom to the work. During the Renaissance, a time of social upheavals, when radical turns of the wheel of fortune brought disastrous local government to the people, forthright public utterings found their way into literature which gave vent to fiery remarks against vainglory, haughtiness, presumptuousness, and tyranny. Godoy enunciates Torres Naharro's sensitive democratic sentiment: "la igualdad/ la loan Dios y la gente" ("equality is praised by people and God") (II, 237, 448–49). Equality among human be ings was a favorite topic of Torres Naharro, as also of others of the so-called Salamancan school of dramatists, such as Encina, Lucas Fernández, Gil Vicente, and other figures less well known. Torres Naharro was outspoken even among friends. Through Godoy, he stated his conviction that "no impide elamistad/ que hombre diga lo que siente" ("friendship does not prevent a man from saying what he feels") (II, 237, 446–47). Plain speaking was a virtue that Torres Naharro clearly believed in and exhibited fearlessly.

In the documentary plays of current events there is no needed compliance with requirements for plot development, for the honor theme, or for characterization. Instead there is a concentrated push for improvement in living conditions for the linguistically disoriented, muted foreigners, wrenched from their diverse lives, and communally deposited in the neglected Roman sculleries. In his satirical, censorious way, Torres Naharro served his inarticulate fellow servants by articulating their eternal longing for a humane exercise of human rights.

V *The Cast*

In the *Tinellaria* the cast totals twenty-two persons, one third of the total number of sixty-five found in all of Torres Naharro's plays. Eleven of these appear in the third act of the *Tinellaria*, a fact which caused Moratín confusion, but which Crawford interpreted as part of the masterpiece of humor (IV, 514). Torres Naharro felt it necessary to include an unusually high number of characters in this play in order to present the variety of persons he found in the *tinelo* with their different styles and conditions of life.

M. Menéndez y Pelayo wrote that there is no one character of central interest in the *Tinellaria*, yet together they leave a strong impression. They are similar to the extent that each reinforces the character of the others. They constitute a collective, group character whose best embodiment perhaps is Barrabás, the unifying force of the first act. Through his whimsical scene with Lucrecia, whom he calls his wife, he shows a picaresque facet of his system of honor. Even his name (often synonymous with that of Satan) suggests evil (III, 462, 170). As a symbolic figure of the *tinelo* his rule is to take whatever he can in order to live as best he can, considering the circumstances. He is a man of his own morality, or more precisely of his immorality, who defrauds those beneath and those above him.

Fraud, deceit, and knavery are the themes the dramatist reiterates as he paints the corruption in the *tinelo*. In conjunction, each character emphasizes the same corrosive vices. They are all rascals working against their superiors, and, when necessary, against each other. The servants are a polylinguistic, immigrant, motley crew. Torres Naharro energetically publicizes the rancorous opinions that stream from the mouths of the characters. They grieve a great deal over their low social status, which some find virtually hopeless; they find fault with the meals, yet they constantly eat and drink, pilfering to supplement their meager rations. The irony is that perhaps the cardinal's wealth could provide enough provisions to permit all to live well, if they only managed the resources properly.[13]

The depiction of woman in this play has not fared as well as in works of Torres Naharro where his pen has run the gamut from the divine to the ridiculous. Woman in *Tinellaria* is a picaresque creature. The washerwoman, Lucrecia, the only female in the *Tinellaria*, is a recognized type found later with similar unseemly attributes in the *Lazarillo de Tormes*. Lazarillo's mother, in order to keep herself and her little son alive takes in washing and lovers with equal abandon.[14]

The *Tinellaria* discloses that there is an overlapping of offices and servant officials in the cardinal's household. It is small wonder that they were stepping on each other's toes and encroaching on each other's territory of command. There was the Mastro, the Despensero, the Escalco, the *credenciero*, and the cook, in that order of importance,[15] followed by a troop of other minor servants including squires, equerries, stable boys, and the like. It was a veritable army of servants that dwelt in the cardinal's palace, without a clearly defined province of authority. Survival being the chief concern, the basic question on their minds with every move was, "What's in it for me?"

All nationals are lightly sketched with no in-depth study of any one group except the Spanish. Among the languages represented are macaronic Latin, French, Italian, Catalan, Portuguese, Castilian, with traces of German and Basque, and there are indigenous dialects of Valencia, Andalusia, and Western Spain. Torres Naharro skillfully handles this mixed linguistic atmosphere wherein the polyglot exchange is often ebullient, effervescent, and always animated.

CHAPTER 9

Comedia Ymenea

W ITH the *Comedia Ymenea* (*The Hymen Comedy*, 1516) we witness the perfection of Torres Naharro's dramaturgy for the fictional comedy. The play is distinguished by dramatic economy with regard to structure, plot, and characterization, and sets the pace for many a play to come.

I *Synopsis*

The rustic prologuist greets his audience on a festive Christmas evening. He seeks the spectators' attention by telling them of a suggestive, erotic escapade which he enjoyed while collecting his pleasures in the pursuit of women. He eventually succumbed to marriage, and his wife gave birth to a child that resembled the local priest. He hopes that the next child will do better and have the looks of the archpriest. In his current extramarital interests, the shepherd is attracted to a girl soapmaker, a flirt who shows a fondness for drink. He met her in midsummer in the vineyard and describes their occasional grappling together. Realizing his loquacity before the audience, the rustic asks pardon and changes the subject, expressing surprise at the cleanliness of the place, and assuring his hosts that he seeks no more than an equitable remuneration for his services. He notes that the five-act play to be presented is not one for generating boisterous laughter, even though it is called a comedy, and then he proceeds to detail its plot.

In act 1 it is late at night. Ymeneo has come to speak to his beloved, Phebea, who scornfully leaves him out on the street without even appearing at her window. Boreas, his accompanying servant, notes that it is time to sleep and suggests that they return to continue their serenading on the morrow. Eliso, a younger servant, also urges Ymeneo to leave because Phebea's brother, the Marqués, comes by frequently with his servants keeping a threatening vigil on

104

Phebea's house. Ymeneo departs and the two lingering servants
agree to flee quickly from any possible danger. Boreas confides to
Eliso that he has fallen in love with Phebea's servant, Doresta, who
to him is as pretty as her mistress. As Boreas and Eliso depart in
search of breakfast, the marquis approaches with his servant-page,
Turpedio. These two are on the alert for Ymeneo, for they know
very well that he frequents the street where Phebea lives.[1] They
think of awakening Phebea, but decide against it, and plan instead
to sleep the remaining portion of the night, perhaps at some girl-
friend's house.

Act 2 occurs later that night. Ymeneo returns with his servants
and hires a group of roaming musicians to serenade his lady. The
tunes stress that no worldly glory can produce joy as great as that
which comes from pining for the beloved. Phebea now deigns to
appear at her window. She has a compassionate heart for Ymeneo
upon his confession of love for her, but is shocked when he asks that
at their next meeting, which is to be the very next evening, she
open the door and give him access to her chamber. He presses on
with his entreaties, brief though they be, and she capitulates to his
desire. He is assured that she will open the door to him when night
comes again.[2] Boreas reminds Ymeneo to tender gifts of gladness to
him and Eliso. Thereupon Ymeneo offers his clothes to them. Eliso
declines the offer, suggesting that it is insane to be overly generous.
Boreas feels obliged to go along with Eliso's suggestion. Ymeneo
appreciates this and promises them something better—the love of a
brother, rather than that of a master. Morning is breaking and they
withdraw, planning to come back later that afternoon. As Ymeneo
departs with his crew, the Marqués in turn comes with his.[3] The
marquis and his lackey know Ymeneo had just been there, and they
plan to catch him that evening when he returns. The Marqués
thinks he will have to kill both Ymeneo and his sister to preserve the
family's untarnished honor. In order to trap the lovers, the Marqués
and Turpedio will sleep through the day, so they can sustain their
vigil all the next night.

In act 3 it is late afternoon. Boreas reprimands Eliso for having
turned down the gifts of clothes that Ymeneo had tendered them
earlier. Eliso is easily convinced now by Boreas of his error, and
agrees to do his bidding in the future. Eliso tries to excuse himself
by terming Ymeneo poorer than they are, stating that eventually
they will fare better when he gets wealthier. Furthermore, Ymeneo

with his faults is still the best master available to them. Boreas insists it is foolish to refuse a gift, and that their obligation is merely to serve well, and for that they are to be paid well. They spot Doresta at the window of her mistress, Phebea, and while Eliso listens, Boreas undertakes to show off his captivating ways with women. Unlike her mistress, Doresta plays harder to get for her beau. Teasingly she considers herself ugly, and flirtatiously questions Boreas' sincerity. Boreas pleads to be treated like his master and to be let in to see Doresta when she opens the door that evening for Ymeneo's rendezvous with Phebea. Stubbornly she resists, until Eliso's disgruntled suggestion for Boreas to give up, suddenly prompts her to change her mind. She agrees to open the door to Boreas, on the condition that it be on some other night. As Boreas and Eliso depart, Turpedio comes beneath Doresta's window and for his part attempts to woo her. She rejects him, indicating that he is a bit young for her. Suggestively he wants to prove to her that he is more of a man than she thinks he is. With sex on his mind, Turpedio angrily withdraws, exchanging threats, insults, and oaths with Doresta.

In act 4 it is the appointed night, and Ymeneo appears with his attendants to keep his rendezvous with Phebea. When he enters Phebea's door, the two servants, fearful of being killed, conspire to flee the scene. In their hasty flight, they abandon a cape which is discovered by Turpedio and Marqués who have come to keep their vigil. Turpedio recognizes the garment of Ymeneo's cowardly servant. Spurred by the knowledge that Ymeneo is with his sister, the marquis wants to enter the house to kill Ymeneo and Phebea, the suspected perpetrators of his family's dishonor. Since they have no key, they know that if they knock, the victims will be warned and will thus escape. Turpedio advises his master to kick the door down, so that without previous warning they will be upstairs before being detected. With swords raised, they leap to the attack.[4]

Act 5 begins with the marquis pursuing and confronting Phebea. Turpedio cautions him to be calm and proceed with prudence. Ymeneo has escaped. The Marqués with sword unsheathed, is about to strike the murderous blow, but directs his sister to confess before his attendant page as witness. Doresta is summoned to witness Phebea's fate. Upon his sister's request, the Marqués agrees to listen to her entire unfortunate tale. Protesting her innocence at first, Phebea seems resigned to death, recognizing her brother's right to kill her, and only regrets not having fulfilled Ymeneo's desires. Attempting to preserve her life, she staunchly maintains that she is free of any crimes, and insists that she did right in loving her husband-to-be. Finally, in desperation, she invokes nature to sympathize with her and through catastrophic earthquakes, eclipses of the sun and moon, and creation of a void of darkness and stillness, to mourn the loss of her innocent life.[5] Terminating her confession, the Marqués announces that her hour of death has come. At that instant, Ymeneo boldly steps into view and halts the execution, declaring that Phebea is his fiancée. When the Marqués objects that a marriage must be arranged by a concerned family member, Ymeneo counters that he himself decides on his wife and needs no help from an intermediary. Similarly, Phebea of her own free will wants to marry Ymeneo. There is little else for Marqués to do but to bless them and let them join hands in matrimony. The retainers who have all returned to the scene declare themselves willing and faithful servants of their new masters. Phebea corrects them, saying that instead of servants they will now become their new brothers and sisters. Doresta is asked to choose Boreas or Turpedio for a husband, but when the issue becomes debatable, Ymeneo takes charge of overseeing a satisfactory marriage for her. As they prepare to visit Ymeneo's home, they join in singing a closing ballad that proclaims, "Victory, victory in love."

II *Analysis*

Literature's importance, besides its aesthetic and moral appeal as entertainment and instruction, can be viewed as the recording of individualized history—of the history of individuals as opposed to the history of states. Literature chronicles the vicissitudes of life on an intimate, passionate, personal level. The *Comedia Ymenea*, like other plays by our author, sets down a small segment of life as possibly lived with its ever-present trials and tribulations during the High Renaissance in Rome or in Naples, as Torres Naharro himself was able to witness it in his own microcosm.[6] The *Ymenea* describes in specific detailed form certain manners, customs, hopes, and concerns of the day.

Vitality of individual action, a collision of intentions with definite challenging aims, is demonstrated by this play, which was probably meant to be performed as part of the wedding celebrations for a member of high society. Judging from the words of the prologuist, the happy occasion took place around Christmas of 1516 (IV, 516) possibly in the palatial household of Cardinal Bernardino de Carvajal, then Torres Naharro's artistic patron (III, 550, n. 156).

This is a major, innovative, interesting, and significant work of the Spanish theater. Till now, except for the Nativity skits and the *Seraphina*, we have been considering documentary plays, plays dealing with current events, the *comedias a noticia*, primarily plotless vignettes of life. This fictional play, a *comedia a fantasía*, has a tightly structured plot. From it a radical new direction is charted for the Spanish stage that catches on with the baroque dramatists. The play is so well structured that it has been compared to those of the seventeenth century, to the classically organized dramas of the eighteenth century, and to the best romantic compositions of the nineteenth century. Truly, it has the essential ingredients that characterize dramatic forms of these several periods, not only structurally, but thematically as well. It is impressive with its night scenes, its ominous muffled street sounds; footsteps scurrying through the perilous streets, and servants flitting about narrow darkened ways casting glances over their shoulders seeking to evade approaching imminent danger. By means of the nocturnal scenes Torres Naharro augments the involving mysteries of suspense while overtones of prankish excitement, typical of Halloween nights, echo through the play. There are the stalking shadows of the night, the warm romanticism of moonlight, the wistfulness of songs and music in the air, and throughout, contrasting with a sense of revelry, hangs the omnipresent danger of death.

Torres Naharro classified the *Ymenea* as a *comedia a fantasía*, one that is imagined, not based on real events, yet retaining a semblance of reality. Its introit is characteristically attuned to a marriage play. Linguistically the prologue appears gross, erotic, and scatologically amusing. Such attributes were expected as part of the pagan invocation of fertility at wedding time. The title of the play and the name of the protagonist, which derives from Hymen, god of marriage, reinforce its intent to celebrate the nuptials. Due to its original contributions to playwriting, the play is one of the most important Spanish dramas written before the time of Lope de Vega, containing characters, themes, and actions that till then had not been documented for the Spanish stage. Its importance and artistic value have been recognized even outside of the Spanish domain. Before 1920 the *Ymenea* had been translated, first into French as *Iménée* by

Angliviel La Beaumelle, and then into English as *Hymen* by H.H. Chambers and A. Bates.[7]

The *Ymenea* is a concise play that could be construed as observing the classical unities, but that matter, as we have seen already in this chapter's notes, is debatable. Though the stakes are enormously high, the plot is simple, reducible to an effort on the part of Ymeneo to win entry into Phebea's home against her brother's violent opposition. Although there is a bifurcation of the action with a secondary plot that parodies the primary love interest, the secondary action is dexterously intercalated with the mainstream of the plot. In the paralleling subaction, Torres Naharro introduces the appealing personage of the *gracioso* and the soubrette in their function as refracted images of their masters. The comic figures embodied in Turpedio and Doresta serve as confidants and alter egos to their masters, contributing hesitant modifying forces to the latters' rash actions. The *gracioso*, like the soubrette, cleverly guides much of the play's plot. Torres Naharro showed true dramatic instinct in the handling of these comic models who certainly were not types in the Spanish drama of his era, but became so during the next two hundred years, and have remained as such to this day.

Torres Naharro takes advantage of the love theme in this urbane comedy and scores telling points on matters relevant to social conditions. Phebea's defensive diatribe before her brother expresses views on marriage that were contrary to the accepted social norms, at least of the preceding generation. Gradually the changing norms gained acceptance among the city dwellers and spread slowly through the rural areas. The attitude of free choice of a marriage mate is present in the pastoral convention of the farces and eclogues of Juan del Encina, Lucas Fernández, and Gil Vicente, wherein the woman is allowed to exercise her own free will in making the important lifelong decisions. In all of the plays of Lucas Fernández where marriage is involved, the parties contemplating it are asked to make their own choices of a spouse.[8] Similar situations are seen in Encina's and Gil Vicente's plays. Though the idea of free choice has been accepted to a varying degree in most societies, it was especially emphasized in literature during the Renaissance period with its stress on individualism.

Along with the challenging matrimonial questions, the defiance of the tyrannical order of relationships between masters and servants also figures in the discussions. Torres Naharro had strong feelings on

this, repeatedly placing a heavy accent on equal, brotherly relationships between master and servant. The audiences both of a particular and a popular nature were conditioned by the general feeling for
equality of mankind. This feeling, originating in pagan times and
gaining new impetus in Christian doctrine, was kept alive by
Spanish dramatists who became spokesmen of the common people's
resurging respect for the individual. The Salamancan school of early
dramatists, Encina, Fernández, and Vicente along with Torres
Naharro affirmed that all human beings were fabricated from the
same clay and were equal sons and daughters of Adam and Eve.[9]

Torres Naharro demonstrates a varied style in the *Comedia
Ymenea*. Critics have consistently acclaimed the play for its intrinsic
values of natural dialogue, purity of taste, lyrical elements, and
careful structuring. In the introit, Torres Naharro uses dialect with
humorous intent, exploiting topics such as sex, scatology, satire of
the clergy, and comic wordplay. In the text of the play, the dialogue
of the masters and the servants alike is simple and smoothflowing,
and the mixed discussions of social or humanistic import are embellished with aphorisms and proverbial phrases. Lyrical passages and
musical interludes mingle with humorous segments to produce the
changes of pace that make this play a most appealing piece of stage
entertainment. In the process, Torres Naharro establishes a completely youthful stage world. The entire play is cast in the environ-
ment of the young, exiling the old who had been present in *La
Celestina*, the inspiring original story for this version.

III   *Sources and Influences*

Of the many studies dealing with the play, one of the most penetrating is that of Miguel Romera Navarro, who notes that this work
represents an extraordinary advance in the evolution of the Spanish
Renaissance theater: "no hay una sola obra que por sì sola re-
presente, como ésta tan considerable avance en el progreso
dramático" ("there is no one work which by itself alone represents,
as does this one, such a sizable advance in dramatic progress").[10]
Granted, Italian theater had already reached a sophistication com-
parable to that of Torres Naharro's play, particularly in the superb
composition of Niccolo Machiavelli's *Mandragola (Mandrake)* and
perhaps in some works of Lodovico Ariosto, both of whom were
Torres Naharro's contemporaries.

Honor is the axis of the *Ymenea*'s plot. Although the marquis may not seem to have been a worthy instrument for the sacrifice of his sister's life, his actions initiated the artistic literary trend which flowered when honor became a main consideration as a basic motif in the baroque theater. The trend in this direction started when Torres Naharro adapted the enormous dramatic possibilities of *La Celestina* and expanded the idea of family honor, forging thereby a largely original plot which placed him in the vanguard of the modern Renaissance dramatists. Through the radical handling of the honor theme and respect for the youthful determination of conjugal choice of mate, this brilliant play established Torres Naharro as an outstanding dramatist without equal in Spain until the age of Lope de Vega.

Torres Naharro distilled and concentrated a portion of the plot from *La Celestina,* lending it important new twists such as the happy ending, the absence of a mediary, and the introduction of the theme of honor, together with the characters of the guardian brother and his confidant servant, all of which attained a long and acclaimed reign in the comedy of the Golden Age. Additional plot innovations incorporated the device of false accusation, exploited as a pivotal point for several of Lope de Vega's and Tirso de Molina's plays.[11] The plot, as has been demonstrated repeatedly by scholars, and chiefly by M. Romera–Navarro, is condensed specifically from acts 12, 14, and 15 of the original sixteen-act version of *La Celestina,* with possible elements as well from the revised acts 1, 11 and 19, of the expanded twenty-one act version of Rojas' work. Gillet and other scholars, including Green and Crawford, have concurred with Romera–Navarro that incidents in the two works for the most part agree.[12] There is a moot question that still challenges scholars concerning the flow of time in both works. Some believe, as we have noted, that the events take place within twenty-four hours,[13] while others have noticed some incongruities in the temporal concept in each work.[14] It is possible that more than one day is covered in the *Ymenea* story.

Speaking of the differences in the two works, Green is correct in observing that significantly Ymeneo "does not make the mistake, does not break the courtly code, as Calisto does in the *Celestina*."[15] There is a promise of fidelity in the *Ymenea* exchanged between Ymeneo and Phebea in Torres Naharro's play and which is a key factor in averting the tragedy that befalls the characters in *La Celestina.* This vow of fidelity before witnesses shifts the action from a tragic to a happy outcome. Ymeneo's intentions, unlike those of Calisto, are determined to have been honorable from the very beginning. He had no desire to seduce the girl without marrying her. The difference in attitude toward the beloved, the desire to possess her in a socially honorable way, that is, through marriage, is stressed in the denouement of the *Ymenea*. Phebea loves Ymeneo as a wife should love her husbnad, not as Melibea loved her inamorato, cherishing desires to be the mistress of Calisto and concurrently rejecting the idea of marriage her parents were planning for her.

The protagonists of both *La Celestina* and the *Ymenea* serve to illustrate the uncanny powers of love that cause men to be not only blind, but deaf and dumb as well. Both males are beside themselves, first altered by the aberrant influence of unrequited love, then by the other extreme of requited love. The deranging power of love is underlined in both works by the repeated use of the word *loco* ("crazy") and *locura* ("insanity"). Yet there is a saving grace that further distinguishes Ymeneo from Calisto. Calisto was incapable of exercising reason to control his passion, or to fulfill his desires in a socially approved manner. In part, what leads to Calisto's downfall is that he followed the course of an unreasonable rebel. He saw only one avenue leading to a solution of his love affair: hiring an intermediary to satisfy his ardor. Ymeneo, on the contrary, states very clearly and deliberately that he is capable of arranging his own love life. Since differing social and religious status may have been an impediment to marriage for Calisto and Melibea, Torres Naharro makes clear that social rank was not a problem for Phebea and Ymeneo. The Marqués acknowledges, "Bien veo que sos yguales/ para poderos casar" ("I see very well that you are equals and thus able to marry") (II, 318, 253–54).

Although scandalous behavior hovers suspiciously above the central characters for much of the play without materializing, there is no sense of sin in Torres Naharro's play, nor is there any intent to reprove lovers consumed with passion. It shies away from such moralizing and concentrates on winsome entertainment. The specter of death haunts the play, but passes on like the other shadows in the night. Without premarital carnal surrender, marriage conducts the lovers safely to a happy ending. Unlike Melibea, Phebea maintains her innocence and thus makes a tragic ending unnecessary. Her long defense of her virtue is impressive and the threatening imminence of death is proved to be unjust. The author seeks pity, compassion, and sympathy for the heroine from the audience. Her stoic insistence on innocence coupled with resigned acceptance of death vividly conjures up liturgical plays on Christ's Passion. Indeed, Phebea's innocence is raised to the level of Christ's as supernatural events are invoked in biblical fashion as proof of her unblemished life.

Along with their differences, there are noticeable similarities of the female protagonists of the *Ymenea* and *La Celestina*. Phebea, like Melibea, regrets having caused suffering to her lover. Although she did not surrender her body to the beloved, Phebea seems to deplore the fact that her own lust was not satisfied before the intrusion of death, "I confess that she errs and sins who tries to thwart the enjoyment of this body which is dust, and before God and you I proclaim my guilt."[16] Both leading ladies have a universally admirable characteristic—that of expressing their will and of clinging to their beliefs, explaining their actions resolutely and unrelentingly in the face of mortal danger. Further conceptual similarities between the two works entail the treatment of the servants by the masters. In each, the master insists on calling his servants "brothers." When rewards are made, they are tendered in articles of clothing. Eliso, one of the servants of the gallant is loyal (like Pármeno, but bewaring of women like Tristán); the other, Boreas, is more experienced, worldly, and selfish (like Sempronio, but falls in love like Sosia). The more experienced, greedy servant successfully corrupts the loyal altruistic one. In both works the retainers prove cowardly, ready to flee from the first sign of danger; conversely, they are boastful of supposed courageous exploits.

Besides the important dramatic source of *La Celestina* there are also proverbial and poetic sources, including ideas found in Jorge Manrique's works and before him in the *Danza de la muerte* (*Dance of Death*). In the *Ymenea*, the Marqués echoes Manrique's lines which proclaim the inevitability of death to all, the rich and the poor, the young and the old alike. In addition to the literary sources for Torres Naharro's work, McPheeters has uncovered real-life incidents in Italy that could have supplied Torres Naharro with material for the avenging guardian-of-honor character of the marquis. He cites the incident of a sixteen-year-old youth who killed his sister's lover a few years prior to Torres Naharro's composition of the *Ymenea*.[17] Torres Naharro's influence carried on into the work of others. Gillet and Green point out that after this play there are subsequent examples of the brother's awesome power of life and death over his wards, "In Sancho de Muñón's *Tragedia de Lisandro y Roselia* (1542), Beliseno has his sister and her lover killed with one arrow as they embrace . . . . In Ruiz de Alarcón's *El Tejedor de Segovia* the protagonist is about to kill his sister to protect her honor" (IV, 519).

It is said that Lope de Vega never acknowledged any indebtedness to Torres Naharro, yet it is very likely that he was familiar with his works and was able to profit by their example. The theatricality of the cape and sword play, the drama of intrigue, became most popular in the theater of the baroque period in Spain. The essentials of the form were crystallized in Torres Naharro's *Ymenea*. Some minor changes were carried out in the succeeding theatrical endeavors, such as reduction of the number of acts from five to three and the development of polymetric versification, but the basic structure and youthful atmosphere of the plays continued unchanged with all the glorious accoutrements of the swashbuckling drama of Calderón. We shall look next at the structure of this play and observe the various aspects that helped to make it such a remarkable piece of work for its time.

IV *Structure*

The *Ymenea* has a relatively simple but highly organized plot which stands as the culminating point of meticulous dramatic craftsmanship in the sixteenth century, its tight construction being clear-cut. In some of Torres Naharro's other plays, acts 2, 3, and 4 vary considerably from each other, with extraneous matters sometimes brought into the story, but the *Ymenea* is carefully planned and executed, proceeding along a genuinely moving path. The exciting theme is insistently kept before the eyes and ears of the audience.

The play has a total of 1968 lines of verse, about two-thirds the length of the baroque plays. The first three acts are approximately of equal length ranging from 300 to 319 lines. Act four is only about half their length (168 lines), while the final act is the longest, with 371 lines. The rest of the 1968 lines are taken up by the prologue material.

The versification is a combination of a twelve line strophic form consisting of six lines followed by a *redondilla* and a rhyming couplet with a short line, or "broken foot." Thus the versification is a line of eight syllables (used earlier only in the *Comedia Jacinta*, 1514–1515), with the rhyme scheme *a b c a b c,* then the *redondilla, d e e d,* and *pareados* (couplets, *ff*), the second last line being short, counting only four syllables rather than the full complement of eight.

The five-act division which Torres Naharro favors was used by classical Roman dramatists and continued in use through the centuries, gaining renewed momentum with the humanists of the Renaissance. After a brief vogue in Spain the five-act structure was first reduced to four, and gradually to three. The five-act structure continued for a much longer period in England, where it was used by Peele, Marlowe, and Shakespeare, among others.[18]

The progression of the play's action commences after its background has been settled and the relationships among its characters have been delineated. Acts 1 and 2 have the expected protasis or expository material with a bonus of foreshadowing of the action to come. The initial act generates the attraction that Ymeneo shows for Phebea, and Boreas for Doresta. Act 2 spells out the protagonist's goal that starts the action rolling. The inciting decision, determined by the leading man, is to request entry to the leading lady's chamber, which in turn triggers the fateful reaction that unleashes the conflict. This occurs when the antagonist Marqués decides to thwart Ymeneo's plans to meet with Phebea in her chamber. The tension grows from then on as the conflict between Ymeneo and the Marqués gradually unfolds. Act 2 thus presents the crucial resolve together with the intrigue as fabricated by the marquis with the help of his servant Turpedio. The strategy is to trap Ymeneo and Phebea in the ecstatic moments of their illicit love. The maneuver is for the Marqués to await Ymeneo in ambush. The inciting decision of act 2 by the protagonists—Ymeneo asking access to Phebea's chambers—is pitted not only against the fateful designs of the antagonistic Marqués, but also needs first to resolve the conflict in Phebea's mind, a minor crisis, for she is not sure she should approve Ymeneo's request. But when she does, and Ymeneo has passed the first hurdle, it is the vengeful brother who casts an alarming shadow over their plans for a rendezvous.

Act 3 serves in part as a delaying interlude, and in part as an undercurrent supporting the main action. This is the act of the servants, in which they attempt to emulate the actions of their masters. The parodying tangentially emphasizes the main plot and at the same time provides a humorous diversion through its treatment of the love affair on the servant level. Minimizing duality of the plot, the dramatist keys in on Doresta as the focal point, the psychological link between the two levels of action and between the two opposing factions. On the one hand she deals with Boreas and Eliso, the servants of Ymeneo, and on the other, with Turpedio, the servant of the Marqués. In this manner the conflict brewing between the opposing forces is kept constantly before the audience, even though the principal characters are temporarily offstage.

Instead of a suspended animation of the main story the plot advances in a bifurcated progression. The epitasis, or planning of the basic conflict, goes forward with little respite even with the diversion. The symmetrical parallelism continues on the lower level as Turpedio becomes angry with Doresta over sex, while his master Marqués becomes angry at Phebea, on their higher level, over honor. Further symmetry is achieved in the plotting as Boreas expects to come to Doresta in the same way that his master Ymeneo will come to Phebea. The counterweight to this is the symmetrical duality of the conflict, as Turpedio will work against Doresta in the same manner that his master, the marquis, will connive against his sister Phebea. The scenic balance extends to the acts and is manifest in the paired entrances and exits of the characters. The entrances are well prepared for, with the characters indicating the specific individual who will partake in the ensuing dialogue. A further symmetry involves the placement of characters on the stage. The third act begins with two servants, Boreas and Eliso; their number is augmented by Doresta, and then the scene concludes with a return to two characters. They are different, however, from those of the first scene of the act, namely, Doresta and Turpedio. In the first and last scenes of the act, there are two persons to carry on the dialogue with additions, subtractions, and changes of personnel taking place in between. The symmetrical balance which is carried on in this act completes the creation of adversaries. As the Marqués is angry at his sister, so Turpedio mirrors his anger with her servant Doresta. The two related camps, females on one side, are tidily divided through anger from the males on the other. At the end of act 3 the lines are clearly drawn: Marqués versus Phebea; Turpedio versus Doresta. The males have also created a schismatic situation with respect to the intrigue. The polarization is set up as: Ymeneo versus Marqués; Boreas and Eliso versus Turpedio.

Act 4 is a direct consequence of earlier decisions which induce the antagonist to build up his case against the protagonist, and the true epitasis, or stretching out, that is, developing of the plot takes place. An intensification of the conflict ensues as the protagonist's plan meets with concerted opposition that results in a recoiling episode within the epitasis. The forging out of the plot continues speedily in this brief act, whose brevity really hastens its action, bringing it to a feverishly suspenseful peak. The concern of the entire play to this point has been with Ymeneo's successful entrance into Phebea's chamber. At this juncture he does achieve his goal, but not without dire complications, a tremendously precarious circumstance as the Marqués charges in for the kill, whereupon the curtain quickly descends. Torres Naharro constructs a perfect curtain to close the fourth act. The story is severed in suspended, violent animation, with opposing contending factions about to meet head-on for the climactic clash. The author has awakened interest, aroused curiosity, and stirred emotions profoundly, charging the air with expectancy, so that the climax is awaited with excitement.

The final act must satisfy the heightened emotions that have been brought to razor sharp edge. How is this satisfaction accomplished? Kicking the door open provides warning enough for the lovers to part and for Ymeneo to leap out to safety. By his escape bloodshed seems at least temporarily avoided. In the absence of the protagonist Torres Naharro prolongs the mortiferous confrontation, converging attention on the antagonist and his sister. The suspenseful gaze is shifted to the sister whose life hangs in the balance of the brother's upraised sword. Phebea pleads innocence and attempts to justify it, becoming introspective of her life when it seems horribly clear that her death is close at hand. Her words have little effect in averting a tragedy, but when the unjust death blow is about to be struck by the marquis, the heroic lover boldly returns. Ymeneo stops the execution with the command, "¡Cauallero, no os mouáis!" ("Do not make a move, sir!") (II, 317, 217). Ymeneo then explains his socially acceptable relationship with Phebea, and as the figure of authority, resolves the plot: he and Phebea will marry, all servants will be treated like brothers and sisters, and Doresta will have a choice of a husband from her two suitors. Although the servants' loves tend to reflect those of the masters, the parallelism on the two levels is not carried out completely, since the servants' marriage is not definitely arranged. Turpedio vigorously resists the

suggestion that he and Doresta tie the knot, and this then anticipates the slightly ambiguous baroque "open-end" closing expressed
in the denouement as Ymeneo proposes, "dexémoslo por agora"
("let's leave it for now") (IV, 320, 340).

For the final scene of this urban comedy, the dramatist brings out
every member of the cast to be appropriately dispensed with. He
thus binds all into a neat package of order once again. A fresh new
status quo is established bringing concord, peace, and harmony.
One hundred years later this same technique of bringing the entire
cast out on stage for the happy closing curtain is used to advantage
by Shakespeare. In fact, this procedure continues to be used when a
dramatist seeks to avoid undue ambiguities and wants to leave his
audience with a strict sense of an ordered universe operating in a
gratifying equilibrium. A happy atmosphere prevails as Ymeneo,
attempting to satisfy the curious imagination of the audience, pre-
dicts a cheerful outcome beyond the confines of the stage action.
The play concludes in exuberance with a happy tune whose verses
proclaim victory in love, indeed, victory over all the obstacles to
love. The song reflects Ymeneo's sentiments cast out reassuringly to
the audience while leading it gradually back to reality out of the land
of exciting fantasy.

Recurring reminders of the plot within the play itself are a novel
contribution by Torres Naharro to the dramatic techniques of the
Spanish drama. The only general summary of the plot occurs in the
preface to this play. Due to the simplicity of the story and the
brevity of the play, the dramatist can accomplish the task of
mnemonic recapitulations by means of rather brief statements
which appear frequently, but irregularly in the text: there are two
recapitulations in act 1, four recapitulations in act 2, one in act 3,
three in act 4, and nine recapitulations in the final fifth act, a total of
nineteen mnemonic references of the story in the *Comedia Ymenea.*
The greatest frequency of recapping statements concentrated in the
last act is the result of critical moments in which the actors need to
identify their relationships to each other and must attempt to justify
the motivation behind their crucial actions. The recapitulations
make it possible for the spectators to accept the reasons, as well as
the significance of the critical events unfolding before their eyes.

In addition to the neatly developed plot, the symmetry in the
acts, there is alternation of the comic and the serious. The play is
further systematically enriched with a considerable amount of lyric

poetry, sententiousness and aphorisms, which along with music underscore the sentiments in the play. The popular songs that garnish the second act express a painful, tormented, suffering love and reaffirm the prevalent emotion of forlorn sadness on the first occasion of the would-be lovers' meeting. The second occurrence of a popular song at the end of the play records the contentment, and testifies to the rejoicing at the favorable outcome. The songs release the lyrical expression enhancing the emotional sense of the play: love is triumphant. Optimism and idealism prevail as an adjustment is reached between love and honor to secure the coming conjugal happiness.

V *The Cast and Characterization*

In this play not only the central episode but also the characters provide the desirable cohesiveness. Renaissance drama, and the period's literature in general, emphasized individuality. Democracy was not a new concept, but emphasis on the individual played an important part in the social growth of the new democracy. Respect for the individual within a state society had been practiced in the periods of democratic government during the classical Greek and Roman ages as well as during the early Christian era. It had a rebirth in the revolutionary age of the Renaissance and the Reformation.

There is genuine characterization in this play. Some of the characters are typed, yet as such they stand out clearly, with individual personalities. The marquis and his servant Turpedio are a felicitous addition to the outline of the Celestinesque story selected by Torres Naharro for his central episodes. They are, besides, a revolutionary contribution to the Spanish theater. Never before him on the Spanish stage was anyone as concerned with family honor as was the Marqués, a self-appointed sanguinary, avenging instrument. A man of action, he was a violent, dissolute creature of the night. With his perplexing, reprehensible double standard, he left his sister unprotected during his nightly escapades, taking liberties for himself which he denied to her. Stands out as a severely narrow-visioned, overly enthusiastic faultfinder, striving zealously to uphold family honor to which he himself could add little. María Rosa Lida de Malkiel detects in the marquis a grotesque reflection of the asceticism of Pleberio from *La Celestina*.[19] Though the marquis is driven solely by the urge to prevent his sister from overstepping her bounds, he has left a memorable mark on the Spanish stage.

Turpedio, attendant page of the marquis serves as alter ego, a confidant who wields a tempering influence on his master. He is the witty voice of moderation, and he is also the organizer of his master's vagaries. In his tacit acquiescence of his master's nightly forays, Turpedio reveals some moral turpitude; yet he remains a positive moral force, curbing the reckless instincts of his master. In the introit Turpedio is aptly described as "osado,/ muy discreto y bien criado" ("daring, very discreet, and well-brought up") (II, 277, 202–3). His literary lineage may be traced back to the running messenger-servant of Roman comedy, who served his master loyally, yet remained argumentative, resourceful, and even scheming.[20] Turpedio is the wisest of the group of servants who appear in the play, humble yet unresentful in his servile station of life. At the same time he can be forceful, capable of anger with his peers, but displaying a generous comprehension of young love. Torres Naharro depicts in him an ingenious foundation of selective innate qualities that molded the *gracioso's* character.

Phebea becomes a character who genuinely engages the reader's sympathy. Turpedio incisively recognizes Phebea's strong nature: "¡Qué donzella/ para burlarse con ella!" ("What a girl to be made fun of!") (II, 285, 263–64). She assumes the role of a martyr when she cowers before her brother's death-dealing hand, expecting even more drastic natural consequences from her tragedy than those which accompanied the crucifixion of Christ. As far as love is concerned, she is a woman of conviction, struggling for individuality, equality, and justice, stubbornly defending her right to love a man of her own choosing: "Mi querer fue con razón/ y si quise, hize bien/ en querer a mi marido" ("My love in reason had its root, and if I loved, I did quite right/ in loving my husband") (II, 314, 124–26). She is a vehement woman of the Renaissance, indeed, a universal woman with stable ideas whose presence is felt in all ages.

Phebea's servant Doresta is loyal and at the same time expediently independent, taking care to assure herself of a suitor in her own right. She holds no envy for her beautiful mistress, perhaps because her suitor declares her to be equally beautiful. Boreas is a flatterer, cynical and cowardly. Worried about economic deficiencies, he considers a man a fool if he can have two capes but is satisfied with only one (II, 298, 40–41). Cheating and lying come easily to him. In the face of danger he prepares to flee and readily expects to justify his flight with a lie, being materialistically selfish and crafty, while Eliso offsets him by his erstwhile idealism and naiveté.

A distinctive aspect of the traditional nature of early Spanish drama, continued in the theater of Torres Naharro, shows up in this exceptional play as well. That aspect is the quick changes of mind within a given character. Such practice of abrupt changes of attitude was established long before it actually shows up in the work of the so-called primitive Spanish playwrights. The tradition of the sudden changes of attitude is perpetuated when a character's belief is easily shattered or readily influenced to flow in another direction. Phebea is an example in point. When her lover entreats her to open the door to him, at first she declines, but then quite suddenly, with just a light spiritual convulsion, as a result of just one more entreaty, she succumbs, "no puedo más resistir" ("I can't resist any longer") (II, 292, 176).[21] In a similar change of heart, Doresta at first rejects the requests Boreas makes upon her to open the door to him, but then, though more hesitantly than her mistress, she does a turnabout in very short order.

The men are just as prone to change their minds as are the women. Eliso, the counterpart of Pármeno in *La Celestina*, does not take as long, nor does he need as much convincing as does the earlier companion of the bawd in relaxing his loyalty to his master. He is inclined to follow the advice of his older companion only too readily. The abrupt changes, frequent in the drama of the early sixteenth century, continued unabated without being considered a deficiency of the genre, until a new realization of psychological sophistication came with the baroque theater.[22]

Torres Naharro served as spokesman for the Spanish community in Italy, blending old ideas with new ones, showing an intense curiosity tempered with bold self-confidence. Despite retaining aspects of the early dramatic genre, in the *Comedia Ymenea* Torres Naharro embellished the simple themes used by Encina and Fernández and provided his compositions with a symphonic fullness and depth not seen since Rojas, and which would not be seen again in Spanish playwrights for almost a century. This work was the last one to be included in the first edition of the *Propalladia* and marked the culmination of Torres Naharro's dramatic art.

CHAPTER 10

Comedia Calamita

T HE *Comedia Calamita* (*The Calamita Comedy*, 1519) returns to the formula that Torres Naharro successfully implemented and implanted in the new Spanish dramaturgy. The basic themes are freshly set and he begins to amplify and modify them with some variations. This play is added to the second edition of the *Propalladia* which appeared in Seville in 1520.

I *Synopsis*

In the introit to the play the shepherd identifies himself as Remojos Pascual, boasts of his skill in games, rustic chores, singing, and dancing, further notes he is in the service of a squire, and is vigorously pursued by girls. This he relates to justify his being selected to come before the audience to introduce a comedy of love in five acts. Before he exhorts the audience to pay close attention to the play, Remojos Pascual goes on to reveal its involved plot.

Act 1 opens with Jusquino, the servant of Floribundo, ruminating that he who does not venture, does not gain. He wants to have a girl friend who can serve as a matchmaker for his master whose beloved is Calamita. Calamita is the sister-in-law of Libina, Jusquino's top choice for a girl friend. Jusquino meets Libina's fool of a husband, Torcazo, and convinces him that he, Jusquino, is Libina's cousin. Torcazo decides that his new "relative" must come to meet and "embrace" Libina, who unbeknown to Torcazo is also a favorite of the town's abbot. When Jusquino does meet Libina, he flatters her, calling her his goddess. But Libina pretends to be cool to him; her experience tells her that men constantly deceive women. Jusquino defends his kind by saying that women are responsible for men's temptations. As Libina leaves, Floribundo appears and professes his love for Calamita. With Jusquino he goes over a letter he plans to send to her, while Jusquino interrupts with facetious remarks. For a price, Jusquino will deliver the letter to Calamita. Upon receiving the desired promise of money, Jusquino feels as rich as he imagines the pope to be.

Act 2 begins with Jusquino complaining about the state of the world. The rich possess everything while he does not get the rewards that he deserves. Jusquino arranges to have Libina deliver Floribundo's letter to Calamita. A student comes who has been teaching Calamita to write. Libina has fallen in love with the student, and a jealous rivalry develops between the student and Jusquino for Libina's affections. Libina fans the fires of jealousy by deceiving the student with the truth, telling him that Jusquino is her new lover. To console the student, Libina arranges to have him return dressed as a woman, whereupon she will introduce him to her husband, Torcazo, as a "cousin" and thus be able to have her "female cousin" share her bed. There is no food in the house, and Libina sends her husband shopping. Enter Phileo, a spy in the service of Empticio, father of Floribundo. He encounters Torcazo returning home with the victuals, and in their conversation it is revealed that Calamita lives with Torcazo and his wife, Libina. Calamita is believed to be Torcazo's sister. Empticio wants his son, Floribundo, to marry a princess of Aragon, and not into Calamita's plebeian family. Phileo tells Torcazo that Floribundo does not want to marry Calamita but only to defame her. Torcazo intends to be on the lookout against Floribundo's nefarious designs, and returns home with the provisions of food, minus a chicken which Phileo "borrows" from him. Phileo suspects that Calamita and Floribundo will manage to marry in secret despite the father's attempts to ward off the marriage. Phileo has no intention to carry out Empticio's insidious plans against Floribundo and Calamita.

Calamita finally appears in act 3, attending mass with her "sister-in-law," Libina. She has received the letter from Floribundo, and wants to complain about his servant, Jusquino, whom she distrusts. Jusquino, who overhears the conversation, thinks Libina should have defended him, and thus when Jusquino sees Torcazo he vengefully informs him that a student is chasing after his wife. When Libina comes home, Torcazo buffets her for keeping company with a student. Libina learns of Jusquino's complicity in this and swears vengeance on him; when she is alone with him, she puts off his advances. The two speak about the letter that Calamita has received from Floribundo, noting that Calamita showed signs of love upon

reading it. Libina goes into the house when Phileo comes down the
street. He confesses to Jusquino that he is spying on him for
Empticio, and the two, as friends, go for a drink in the nearest
tavern.

In act 4 Empticio reminisces with his son Floribundo about how
good his son used to be and how he has now turned against his father
because of a woman. Floribundo assures his father that he will not
commit any foolish act. In the next scene of this act Torcazo relates
how noisily and boisterously his wife's "cousin" (in reality, as we
have seen, a student dressed in the guise of a woman) sleeps with
her. Torcazo, for his part, has sensual designs on the "cousin." But
as he dares to assault "her" he discovers that "she" is wearing trou-
sers under her dress. The ingenious student-"cousin" cleverly calls
this a miracle that divine providence has provided to save "her"
from the beastly clutches of Torcazo. Later, Libina speaks with
Calamita who confides her wish to be Floribundo's wife. When he
comes, they exchange promises of marriage before Libina as witness, and are overheard as well by the eavesdropping Jusquino, who
seeks out Phileo and tells him of the marriage vows. The latter
promises to protect Jusquino from the expected wrath of Empticio,
when he learns of his son's surreptitious marriage to a woman whom
Empticio considers to be the illegitimate child of a "bad abbot."

In act 5 Floribundo soliloquizes about the type of woman best
suited for him as a wife—one that brings peace to his home and no
more, because he already possesses wealth and all that goes with it.
He has heard that Calamita comes from a good family and hopes that
his father will be happy with the marriage. As he sees three people
approach, he hides. It is his father and the two servants, Jusquino
and Phileo, all of whom at the behest of his father come ostensibly to
kill Floribundo for the bad marriage his father feels he has just
contracted.

They see Torcazo, homeward bound, and Jusquino decides to
play a trick on Torcazo and his wife. He summons Torcazo and tells
him to test his wife's love by pretending to be dead. Torcazo lays
down at the door of the house, and when his wife discovers him
"dead" she pretends to cry. Her student-lover happens along and
tells Libina she should not cry over a "jackass" and that if she is
widowed, he himself will marry her. Torcazo can not contain himself
and "returns" to life. The student flees, while Libina, "relieved" to
see her foolish husband alive, reenters the house with him.

Jusquino and Phileo laugh at foolish Torcazo's antics, but soon begin to wonder why Floribundo has not come out of Calamita's house. The father remains adamant about his scheme to take his son's life. Trapaneo, Torcazo's father, returning home from his most recent trip to Sicily where he had been reaping grain, reveals that he had worked for Empticio over twenty years ago. The putative father of Calamita, Trapaneo divulges her true background: She is really the daughter of a Sicilian noble couple. At birth, to save her life, Calamita was switched for a male child born to a shepherdess. Prior to her birth, Calamita's father in his yearning for a son had threatened to have a female child killed, as his wife had already given him five daughters. Trapaneo helped the mother to switch the babies. Acting as the messenger and carrier of the exchanged children, he managed to keep Calamita and to raise her as his own child. A few years later, all the noble family's children, including the shepherdess' son, perished in a plague and only Calamita now remained of the family. Torcazo and Libina are reduced to "adopted relatives," and the news of Calamita's noble birth facilitates Empticio's acceptance of his son's marriage to her. Floribundo forgives his father for having sought to punish him with death. Jusquino concludes the play by bidding the audience to retire to sleep, for the official public wedding will take place only on the following day.

II *Analysis*

The *Comedia Calamita,* written after the *Comedia Ymenea,* was first published in the second edition of the *Propalladia* (1520). From a literary viewpoint, the *Calamita* is Torres Naharro's next best composition after the *Ymenea.* With 2796 lines, it is also one of his longer plays. As befits a fictional comedy, fame, love, and honor are among its preoccupations. The play may have been presented first in Seville, a tentative conclusion drawn simply from reference to the "gradas de Sevilla" ("the gradins of Seville") (III, 684, 373), identified with the city's cathedral. Suspense is resolved through anagnorisis, and a *deus ex machina* device, "lo ha traydo Dios" ("God has brought him") (II, 455) provides the desired satisfactory conclusion.

The play, in couplets of *pie quebrado,* is written clearly, with the interrelationships of the cast always specifically delineated. This permits the appreciation of motives and actions of the characters, and of anticipating with satisfaction what is to take place on stage. Technically, the story is well planned. The author reveals his own awareness of the plot when it progresses well, "Bien se va ardiendo esta trama" ("This plot is coming along well") (II, 387, 346), or when it slows down, "¡O, qué prolixo sermón!" ("Oh, what a prolix discourse!") (II, 452, 478). This contrasts with his unsure self-awareness in the *Comedia Soldadesca* where he apologetically mentions the possibility of imperfectly organized events (II, 144, 107).

At the play's beginning, the speaker of the introit is depicted with one of Torres Naharro's standard devices, that of forgetfulness; boasting and eroticism which are equally standard. Acts 1 and 2 provide the exposition, mixing a few brief humorous scenes that delay the embroiling of the plot till the third act. From the early dialogue the name of Calamita is at the forefront of attention so that the audience is well prepared, perhaps overly so, for her late appearance on stage at the onset of act 3. From the third act on, the complications succeed one another rapidly. This type of plot development continues through minor crises and complications, until the approach of the climactic point which comes late in the final act.

After the climactic scene, when chaos gives way once again to order, we have the expected resolution, cleverly arranged in the last hundred lines, thus maintaining a suspenseful interest to the very end. Meanwhile, the play has been kept from degenerating into tension-ridden weariness by the intercalation of humorous incidents along the way. There is no real intertwining of a main plot and a secondary one in which the actions of the upper level of society would be reflected in a subplot of lower-class figures as in the *Ymenea*. Actually, we find here only a main plot in which both the upper-level protagonists and those of the lower class combine their efforts to achieve one desired solution. All characters are involved in either effecting or impeding the marriage of Floribundo and Calamita. In lieu of a bona fide subplot there are interrupting incidents of comedy, which in some manner serve to propel the plot on its way.

The *Comedia Calamita* is one of two plays that Torres Naharro's contemporary Juan de Valdés singled out for praise in his discussion of Spanish writers. He was particularly pleased by Torres Naharro's clear unaffected style: "es muy llano y sin afectación ninguna, mayormente en las comedias de *Calamita* y *Aquilana*" ("it is very plain and without any affectation, especially in the comedies of *Calamita* and *Aquilana*").[1]

This drama extends and varies the themes conceived for the *Ymenea*. Not only do we find love and family honor closely interrelated, but a continuation of the formulas for humor conducted through the *gracioso,* and concretization of standards for cohesiveness of the play through prefigurations and recapitulations; all this is sprinkled with social awareness suggesting that Torres Naharro was cognizant of having created a successful theatrical formula in the *Ymenea* that could be exploited profitably before cosmopolitan Spanish audiences.

M. Menéndez y Pelayo sees in the *Calamita* an intrigue of the type found in *I Suppositi (The Betrothed,* 1508) of Ariosto.[2] This play of love was performed in the Vatican in 1519 with stage decorations painted by Raphael. In both plays a student attempts to conquer his beloved through the ruse of a disguise; both likewise contain an anagnorisis, a recognition scene. In the *Calamita* the anagnorisis entails a maiden, and in *I Suppositi* the leading man. In each case the characters involved are of Sicilian origin and both plays end in marriage. Ariosto continued this formula in his *Il Negromante (The Necromancer,* 1520), which also exhibits assumed names, disguises, anagnorisis, and marriages.

Green, following A. Lenz and R. L. Grismer, has additional ideas on the source for the plot, which he sees as coming from *Heautontimorumenos* by Terence (IV, 536). Green also connects a few humorous incidents to *Calandria,* an Italian comedy by Cardinal Bibbiena (1514). The *Calandria* contains kidnappings, disguises, love, and a double wedding—incidents not unlike those of the *Calamita.* The *Calandria* was played in honor of Isabella d' Este in Rome. Bartolomé de Torres Naharro may have seen this performance and thus acquired some ideas from it for his work (IV, 536).[3] Besides these three possible sources, there are some similarities also with *La Celestina,* attributable to a burlesque vein that attempts to parody the trite fad of courtly love. There can also be detected parallelism with certain farcical episodes from Boccaccio's *Decameron.* And, finally, as in so much of Torres Naharro's work, there are profound marks on his poetic sentiments toward life and death that are traceable to concepts enshrined in the *Couplets* of Jorge Manrique.

III *Structure*

The device of prefiguration is utilized from the early prefatory remarks when the introit speaker informs spectators that the play has a five-act structure. Indeed, he prepares the audience to count them. The same speaker adds that there will be a marriage at the end; and as the wedding vows happen not to be performed on stage,

the forewarning is well made, for it tells the audience of the resolution to the play.

The author achieves some reassuring foreshadowing as Jusquino
emphasizes to Libina that Calamita's honor will not suffer by his and
his master's visits. This foreshadowing is to be remembered, "que
su honra ni su fama / no valdrá menos por nos" ("for neither her
honor nor her fame will be lessened by us") (II, 487, 341). At the
end of act 1 the stage has been set for the intrigue that will lead to an
eventual happy conclusion.

More background to the action is presented in the second act
along with further prefiguration by the other servant of Floribundo's
family, Phileo, a confidant for Floribundo's father, Empticio. Phileo
reiterates the happy outcome for the young lovers. He announces
that his old master in his effort to thwart their happiness, "por cierto
en gran fantasía / se ha metido, / no ganará en el partido" ("certainly
has placed himself in great phantasies, he will not win in the game")
(II, 400, 233–35). Despite statements to this effect, the playwright
manages to awaken a series of doubts by comments such as
Empticio's to his son: "aurás de ser mi tormento" ("you will be my
torment") (II, 424, 51). This prefiguration of necessity leads to a
dead end, being one that is not materialized. Several other false
prefigurations sow doubt as to the outcome, thereby arousing suspense. Prefiguration meant to go astray is exemplified by several
incidents, but in particular by the designs expressed by Empticio
that his son Floribundo would be better off dead than improperly
married (II, 441, 11). With his servants he waits in ambush to kill his
wayward son, but despite this attempt to fulfill the prefiguration,
the foreshadowing of the killing goes astray. It must, if the playwright is to save his avowed happy conclusion, but without this false
foreshadowing of Floribundo's death, a substantial amount of interest, conflict, and suspense would have been lost.

The main course of the action, fully summarized in the introit, is
further partially summarized at several steps along the way to its
climax. These timely recapitulations, inserted to keep the audience
abreast of what is happening on stage, signal basic elements of the
plot which one might call "dramemes."[4] Where do these important
recapitulations come, and who gives them? The answer to this double question provides an appreciation of the playwright's technique
and of his full awareness as to basic dramatic essentials.

The first recapitulations of the main components of the action,
that is of the "dramemes," understandably come toward the conclu-

sion of the first act. Some key events have transpired that need to be recalled. When Jusquino is alone on stage he recapitulates these and then projects future outcomes: "Ya me hize su pariente del villano, / tengo a Libina en la mano / y ella al moço en las entrañas; / vsaré de tales mañas / que presto te daré sano" ("I've already made myself a relative of the rustic, I have Libina in hand, and she has the youth in her entrails; I'll use such wit that soon you'll be healthy") (II, 392, 515–19). Thus the act draws to a close with a recapitulation, and at the same time with an anticipatory statement.

The playwright has set the play up well in his first act. Before the curtain of the second act rises, there is a chance that during the hiatus the spectators may have forgotten what has happened, and, moreover, there may even be some late arrivals who need to be told what they have missed. Consequently, in the first seventy lines of act 2, Torres Naharro presents another recapitulation coinciding with the action of the first *jornada*. Jusquino begins the recapitulation with the denoting words, "Ya sabes . . ." ("You already know") and confirms that his master loves Calamita (II, 395, 54), adding a recapitulation of the relationships between Torcazo, Libina, Jusquino, and Calamita (II, 403). There is little furthering of the plot, because this act deals primarily with relationships between the characters and recapitulation of the plot.

In the third act, the audience is expected to be well aware of the situation; the playwright attempts no additional recapitulations. The action goes on, as prefigured initially with Jusquino's scheming now in full swing. The fourth act offers additional molding of character, but the action begins to gather momentum. Still, characterization seems to be the main function of this act. There is but fleeting, false recapitulation as Empticio states that Calamita "es hija de vn mal abad" ("is daughter of a bad abbot"), and at this juncture objects to Floribundo's marrying her (II, 424). Empticio's objection becomes the moving dramatic force henceforth for the conflict in the play. This fourth act proves to be the principal act for the intrigue which has been awaited since the initial exposition and the continuing buildup through the comic second act, and the characterization of act 3. There are two instances of immediate recapitulation of action that just preceded: one deals with the lustful approach by Torcazo to his wife's "cousin," the other with the exchange of marriage vows of the two lovers.

In the fifth and final act, Floribundo speaks of the virtues of his wife. This is clearly intended as a reminder to the audience of the marriage that has taken place in the preceding *jornada*. In act 5 some prefiguration is closely allied to the function of recapitulation: as Empticio plans to kill his son to abbreviate the bad marriage which his son has contracted (II, 441, 115). Similarly, the playwright employs the related device of reiteration, by which we understand an immediate repetition of an isolated event. Instead of summarizing the long-range plot as does recapitulation, reiteration occurs in the last act as Torcazo comes on stage and indirectly informs all that he and Jusquino are "relatives," by addressing him with "¿D´vas, mi primo, Jusquino?" ("Where are you going, my cousin, Jusquino?") (II, 443, 194). Torres Naharro avails himself of the devices of prefiguration and recapitulation repeatedly, assigning the tasks to any character, primary (as Jusquino) or secondary (as Empticio), whenever the action requires a justification of motivation.

IV *The Cast*

M. Menéndez y Pelayo says that the *Calamita* is a comedy of intrigue of the neoclassic type wherein the characters' names seem to come from the repertory of Ariosto or Plautus.[5] The characters do bear names with a mixture of classical Greek and Latin flavor. Calamita is "lodestone," which can be used as a synonym for love, inasmuch as the object of love attracts like a magnet. In addition, the name could be related to "calamity" or to the unfortunate history of Calamita from her birth until the beneficent conclusion of the play when her fortune changes drastically for the better with her marriage to Floribundo. Floribundo derives his name from "flower of the world" (the name is reminiscent of Floristán in the *Seraphina*); Phileo in Greek means "fond of self." Unlike his sobriquet, Phileo is quite kindly, fair-minded, a good friend, and not really preoccupied with self-love. The other servant, Jusquino, is a little more difficult to associate with his name. If the name is related to Greek 'νσγινον ("húsginon") its meaning would suggest the color "scarlet" perhaps referring to his fashion of dress. With respect to Empticio's name, if it comes from Greek, Euticio, as it appears in one of the editions of the *Propalladia*, then it could conceivably come from 'εμτθχης ("heutúches") meaning "lucky." He is lucky indeed, despite his occasional self-pity. Trapaneo derives his name from the city of Trapana, modern Trapani, capital of Sicily, which he frequents on reaping expeditions. Libina possibly is derived from

Libitina, the Italian goddess of voluptuous pleasure.[6] Truly, Jusquino considers Libina to be his goddess (II, 382, 185). Torcazo is a
word standing for *tonto* ("fool") in Spanish and still so used in Colombia. *Escolar* is another Spanish term used generically for the
rascally student. Finally, although it is not usual for the introit
speaker to have a name, this monologuist is called Remojos Pascual.
The first name is ludicrous, suggesting a drinker, and the second is
typically rustic, related to the shepherds of Encina and Lucas Fernández.

Beyond the use of charactonyms the following characters are introduced in the first act: Jusquino, Torcazo, Libina, and Floribundo,
in that order. In just two lines Libina's character is delineated as
loose, light-headed, and happy, when her husband claims that she is
"del cura toda entera / tan querida" ("so wholly beloved by the
priest") (II, 380, 113–14). Later, this is emphasized when we learn
that she visits the abbot as well! Libina herself claims that men
constantly deceive women, but ironically, she constantly deceives
her simpleton husband with many men. Although Floribundo is an
impetuous young man, impatient in his desires and extravagant in
speech, claiming that his unrequited passion causes him greater
torment than can be felt by the greatest sinner in hell, and so
reckless that he hands over to Jusquino the key to his strongbox, he
does not exhibit the morbid weakness that frequently reduces
Calisto in *La Celestina* and the characters modeled on him to physical or mental imbecility. Strength of character is exhibited by
Floribundo in the fourth act when he defends his honorable intentions in his love for Calamita and expresses his own philosophy of
free will in choosing a wife, maintaining his right to a personal
choice of a mate.

The heroine retains control over her emotions, giving no signs
that she has passions that conflict with prudence. Calamita possesses
nobility of character to accompany her noble birth. She is determined not to be seduced, and correspondingly is angry when her
sister-in-law acts as the agent of a would-be seducer, and while she
may have succumbed to Floribundo had he shown the requisite
persistence and guile, she yields only when she has arranged for a
marriage far more advantageous than a woman of her ostensible
social position might expect. Although Torres Naharro gives
Calamita an aura of respectful authority over the servants and her
lover, he does not endow her with any extraordinary grace of beauty

in speech or action. No new moods are revealed in the course of the play in her, and at its conclusion she is no different from the sketchy picture presented prior to the third act. She professes no different ideas from those held upon her first entrance. She is steadfastly and consistently portrayed as a woman in love, awaiting her opportunity to tie the knot with her lover. She does succeed in achieving what she was after—marriage with Floribundo, but this is done more through his efforts and through those of the servants than through hers.

The greatest buildup of characterization comes as Empticio speaks of the character of his son Floribundo. The latter has been most obedient, in fact a model son till now: "niño me solías ser obediente,/ y al maestro reuerente/ y de Dios muy temeroso,/ tras los vizios perezoso,/ tras la virtud diligente" ("You used to be an obedient child, and respectful of teacher and fearful of God, slow for vices, diligent after virtue") (II, 424, 29–34). Floribundo adds to this, "me aueys fecho/ hombre complido y derecho" ("You have made me a proper and polished man") (II, 425, 90–91). The good upbringing of Floribundo, temporarily tarnished in his father's eyes, surfaces again when at the play's conclusion he understandingly comments on his father's concern for him, to the point of accepting his father's unnatural desire to kill him rather than tolerate disgrace to the family's honor through a bad marriage: "Padre, razón te movìa" ("Father, reason moved you") (II, 455, 592). Despite this buildup, Floribundo, along with Calamita, remains among the least developed characters. Both are nebulous and depend upon a reader's knowledge of conventional stereotypes, of leading man and lady, for their contribution to the motivating forces in the plot. On stage, of course, costuming and outward appearance would add the needed dimensions to their characters in order to make them vibrate fully with life. The supporting characters by contrast accentuate the virtues of the protagonists. The secondary characters have animalistic designs on members of the opposite sex, while the two protagonists ennoble their love by following courtly ideals.

Yet the prime mover of the action in the play is a secondary character. Jusquino schemes to bring about the goals of Calamita and Floribundo. Consequently, he is the best delineated character, with a fuller presentation of his personality than the other characters. He is an excellent example of the full-fledged confidential servant who serves his master and at the same time tries to obey the opposing interests of his master's father. He serves as adviser to his master and parodies his love by loving the confidante of his master's lady. The qualities of this confidant-servant are subsequently reflected in many of the *graciosos* of the baroque Spanish drama. Jusquino is vital to the plot in the *Comedia Calamita* as the directing force of the play. His function is that of a director: he opens the play, plans all the strategy, and ends the presentation with a final speech to the spectators: "Sus, sus, noble compañía./ Sé que a nos/ vence el sueño como a vos;/ ya estaréys de mala gana./ Las bodas serán mañana;/ yd con la gracia de Dios" ("Up, up, noble company. I know that sleep is overcoming you just as it is us; you must be tired; so leave with the grace of God.") (II, 455, 593–98).

Torres Naharro attempts to motivate and justify events in the play. Although there are occasional chance and coincidental meetings, others are deliberately set up by the dramatist. When Libina discovers that there is no food in the house and sends Torcazo out to obtain some, the scene is set for the visit between her and Jusquino, as well as for the scene in which Phileo encounters Torcazo homeward bound. Thus the dramatist launches a humorous scene and promotes the progression of the plot's complications.

V *Humor*

The ribald comedy in the *Calamita* is the most risqué in the works of Torres Naharro, and depends to a large degree on exploitation of sexual overtones. The roles of the disguised student and jealous husband belong to the lower levels of Italian comedy of Lodovico Ariosto (1474–1533) and to the clever stories of Boccaccio (1313–1375). The comic scenes have the scintillating wit found later in Lope de Rueda's *pasos* or Miguel de Cervantes' *entremeses*. Torcazo, like the simpletons of Lope de Rueda, is natural, friendly, extremely warm, and pitiable, appealingly funny, for he is the victim rather than the perpetrator of practical jokes. Sex works for Torres Naharro as a joke in the same way that it does for Cervantes.[7]

Along with this type of humor, a sharper satirical vein, rooted in social tensions, is directed at the clergy whose wealth had become proverbial. The clergy exhibit overzealousness for women. Libina visits the abbot frequently and is friendly with the priest. Similarly, the ever dependable comic figure of the sexton helps to heighten the lasciviousness of the priest whom he serves as a procurer. Further satire of the clergy becomes even more biting as their promiscuity leads to numerous offspring from their concubines, one of them "es tan pura / 'hija de abad' su figura / qu' el cabello se me eriza; / porque los que más baptiza / diz que son hijos del cura" ("her figure is so purely 'daughter of the priest' that my hair stands on end; they say that the majority of those he baptizes are his kids") (II, 407, 420–24). Torres Naharro's scoffing anticlerical sentiment was a scathing reflection of the prevailing corruption which not only the laity, but even members of the clergy itself, found necessary to condemn.

We conclude this chapter with Green's well chosen words. Completing Gillet's posthumous *Torres Naharro and the Drama of the Renaissance*, Green wrote, "From the standpoint of its contribution to the development of the *comedia* of the Golden Age, the [*Comedia*] *Calamita* may be regarded as an advance toward that *ingeniosa fábula de España* ["ingenious fable of Spain]—the *comedia de capa y espada* ["cape and sword play"]—with its comings and goings, its suspension and renewal of the action, its ever forward movement, its introduction of extraneous scenes for purposes of entertainment. But the *comedia de capa y espada*, at its best, is more than a comedy of intrigue; it is a wonderland of delight, lyrical drama of a high order, wherein baseness is magically transmuted into gold . . ." (IV, 537).

CHAPTER 11

Comedia Aquilana

THE *Comedia Aquilana (The Aquiline Comedy*, 1520–1523) is Torres Naharro's last published play. It appears in the third edition
of his collected works, issued in Naples in 1524. His theatrical formula is expanded as he employs its various devices, and as in the
Calamita, intermingles experimental variations into its basic themes
of love, honor, and comedy.

I *Synopsis*

The shepherd greets the audience and the newlyweds together
with their attendants. Apologizing for his rustic talk, he notes that it
is of the type used in similar festivities. Speaking of his late love,
Luzía, he utters coarse expressions and obscene allusions relating to
his unsuccessful sexual advances to her. She was a woman of enormous manlike features, but nevertheless, he feels pangs of remorse
for her loss. He then recalls his mission to the audience, and proceeds to recount the plot of the wedding play.

The first act opens on a moonlit night in Spain. Aquilano appears
disguised as a squire, although he is in reality a Hungarian prince, a
fact known only to his loyal servant Faceto, whom he cherishes like
a brother. Faceto is asked to read Aquilano's letter from Felicina,
whom Aquilano loves dearly, desiring to win her love on his personal worth, rather than on any attractions of his lineage. Faceto
teases Aquilano by comic misreadings of the letter. The missive sets
up a rendezvous for Aquilano and Felicina between midnight and
one o'clock. Faceto laments the fact that he must serve loyally a
young man whom love has made lose all reason. Thinking of his own
situation, he realizes it would be desirable to enjoy life more fully
before old age and death creep upon him. Accordingly, he plans to

emulate his master, choosing Dileta to be his girl friend. She is not beautiful, he concedes, but good enough to bed with.

Master and servant approach Felicina's window and Aquilano sends his words of courtly love in her direction. His lady has been both unjust and unkind to him while he is being consumed by the flames of love for her, yet satisfaction comes from thinking of how blessed is his illness that awaits a cure from her. Belatedly, Felicina appears at her window, anxious to play her role as the object of courtly love. Consumed with true love, she affects haughtiness, because her station in life, as she sees it, is higher than Aquilano's. Preoccupied with her honor, she is wary of betrayal, yet arranges for Aquilano to come to her in secret the next day. Faceto overhears the entire conversation and reminds his overjoyed master that it is time to relinquish their vigil.

In act 2 the gardeners, Galterio and Dandario, awake unsure whether it is a working day or a holiday. Unable to resolve their doubt, they launch into a series of reciprocal insults until hunger calls them to breakfast. A new discussion breaks out in which they stress their own democratic sentiments and express little esteem for their king. Dandario equates himself to the king, asking "quánta ventaja me lleua?/ Ambos somos de vn metal,/ y hijos de Adám y Eua" ("What advantage does he have over me? We're both of the same metal, and sons of Adam and Eve") (II, 492, 137–39). He passes on to the subject of the humility of Christ and the theme of *gloria mundi* ("glories of the world") that must pass on. Galterio agrees and in a philosophical digression they find greater happiness in their poverty than have lords and kings in their affluence. When about to return to their huts for breakfast, Dileta, Felicina's maid, calls after them to inquire about the whereabouts of Faceto, and leaves a message to have him meet her. As the two gardeners launch into the matter of how to greet a woman properly, Galterio becomes rather risqué in his imagined actions with a woman like Dileta. Their brief venture into salacious humor is truncated by Faceto's appearance. They give him Dileta's message, exit, and he helps himself to the fruit in the garden. Awaiting Dileta at her window, Faceto contemplates how he would like to spend his time with her. When Dileta appears, Faceto wants access to her room. She resists, but reminds him to tell Aquilano that the latter is expected to come to Felicina alone and early. Faceto persists in seeking favors for himself, and Dileta finally agrees to receive him, provided he will behave.

Act 3 opens on the second night. Felicina confesses to Dileta that she is passionately in love. Impatiently, she awaits Aquilano's arrival for their appointed rendezvous. Dileta urges Felicina to be more liberal of herself, but Felicina is concerned with her honor, which she realizes is all too easily lost and much too difficult to recover. Aquilano makes his entrance, vowing that he would be happy to exchange one year of his life for one hour's service to Felicina. Felicina, alerted by unexpected sounds and fearing discovery of her relationship with the commoner, Aquilano, tells him to withdraw. Aquilano's heart, weakened with love, can not bear this rejection, and he collapses on the spot.

The gardeners, sleepily approaching, discover footprints and fear that a thief has entered; hearing moans, they think them to be from a departed cleric's soul, and begin an incantation to conjure it. Pursuing the moaning, they stumble upon Aquilano under a tree. He rejects their offers to help, and seeks death, explaining the hopeless state of his fatal illness. While Dandario runs off to summon the king, Galterio remains beside Aquilano to comfort him in his final moments. Seeking to make peace with himself, Aquilano enunciates his testament: he offers his money to Galterio, his soul to God, his body to earth, and his heart to Felicina. Galterio, unable to understand Aquilano's manner of speech, criticizes the fancy courtly language. Meanwhile, Aquilano falls asleep and soundly snores, giving Galterio an idea that it is a good time for him to take forty winks as well.

In the fourth act Dandario returns with King Bermudo, who laments the ill fortune that is taking from him his only chance for a son. Bermudo, having given up hope of a son of his own, has looked upon Aquilano as one who might even be worthy of taking his place someday as ruler of the kingdom. Bermudo calls upon his best physicians to cure Aquilano's malady. Galterio suggests the best doctor he knows—a veterinarian who cured his donkey. The rustics extol the virtues of local quacks who customarily attend to their illnesses. Three royal physicians answer the call: Galieno, Polidario, and Esculapio. Bermudo promises them whatever they desire, if they can cure Aquilano. The doctors discuss the symptoms but disagree on the diagnosis. The youngest, Esculapio, who has a beautiful young wife, suggests that Aquilano is suffering from melancholy, a broken heart, and that this can be ameliorated by parading beautiful women of the palace before him. Thereby his affection can also be pinpointed, and the object of his love discovered. The rustics naively suggest that some of the village wenches should likewise be brought in to participate in the parade of beautiful women. Esculapio demands that all leave the place and the parade of the young ladies begin; he watches Aquilano's expression and feels his pulse as the women pass before him, reporting then to Bermudo that Aquilano loves Esculapio's beautiful wife. When Bermudo offers to compensate Esculapio for his wife if he gives her to Aquilano as a cure, Esculapio rejects the offer saying that neither his honor nor his wife are for sale. Attempting to convince Esculapio to cede his wife to Aquilano, the king asserts that he would be happy to offer his own daughter if she were the cause of Aquilano's melancholy. Esculapio has awaited precisely this turn of events and hastens to inform Bermudo that this is indeed the case—that Aquilano loves Felicina. Bermudo, who is disturbed at the thought that his daughter, a princess, is loved by a commoner, judges Aquilano an ingrate for having been raised in Bermudo's palace and yet falling in love with his daughter, thereby tarnishing his regal honor. Aquilano admits that Bermudo has a right even to kill him but insists that his daughter is none the worse for having been adored by Aquilano. Aquilano is ready to die, and Bermudo now assumes the role of consoling him in his final agony. Aquilano meekly, though dutifully as a son, attempts to strengthen Bermudo in his own approaching hour of grief.

Faceto, who wishes to speak with Bermudo, interrupts the agonizing moments of Aquilano. Haltingly and with annoying delaying incidents that rouse the anger of Bermudo, Faceto reveals that Aquilano is the crown prince of Hungary to whom Bermudo had intended to marry off his daughter six years earlier. It was then that Aquilano, hearing reports of Felicina's beauty, fell in love with her and, disguised as a squire, had sought her out to win her true love for himself. King Bermudo is naturally happy to learn of this fortuitous change of circumstance, and all go in search of Felicina who holds the key to Aquilano's cure and her own happiness through marriage.

Act 5 shows a desperate Felicina calling upon her irreconcilable fortune for help. Unfulfilled and betrayed by love, she seeks refuge in death, believing that her lover is dying; without him her life is

meaningless. Had she been a man, Felicina feels she would have
ended her miserable life already. After sending Dileta away, she
seeks a branch from which to hang herself, but discovers that she
can not make the necessary knot in the rope for the noose. She then
meditates on alternate ways of suicide. Perhaps she can stab herself,
or jump off a tower. As if by divine will, Dandario appears and she
sends him for a knife. But having forgotten to tell him to bring a
sharp one, Dandario thwarts her plans when he returns with a
worthless knife. Depressed, she regrets having been harshly discourteous to Aquilano. Dileta in an exalted mood, bursting with
marvelous news for Felicina, returns unwittingly to hamper a further
suicide attempt. Hoping to make the most of this unique situation,
she asks for a reward for the glad tidings she brings. Felicina, in no
mood for such things, warns her maid that she will strike her instead, if she does not leave her alone. Dileta reports enormous
rejoicing everywhere. When Felicina is convinced that there really
is some great news in the air, namely, that Aquilano will survive,
she falls prey to Dileta's designs. Bent upon enjoying her moments
of glory, Dileta extracts an apology on bended knee from Felicina
and, adding insult to injury, demands that Felicina kiss her hand;
finally, the mistress must serve Dileta, however briefly, as a
lady-in-waiting. Objecting to all three humiliating demands,
Felicina nevertheless concedes. After these delaying actions Dileta
recounts the secret that Faceto has already divulged, one that by its
sheer revelation saved Aquilano's life. Faceto unmasked Aquilano's
true identity as the prince of Hungary, heir to its throne. Felicina
and Dileta are then discovered by the searching crowd as Faceto
and the rest of the cast rushes onstage. Aquilano, recovering his
health, is told by the jubilant King Bermudo to embrace Felicina as
his new bride, and Faceto concludes the play, proclaiming to the
audience that the wedding of the lovers will take place on the morrow.

II *Analysis*

The *Comedia Aquilana* is considered to be the first known romantic play written for the Spanish theater. Similarly, the *Calamita* is
considered to have been the first Spanish play of intrigue, as the
Ymenea is the first play of the dashing, cloak-and-dagger variety. As
a matter of fact, all three plays share much the same elements of
romanticism and intrigue in varying degrees of intensity. The date

of *Aquilana* is conjectured, by Gillet, with considerable doubt, to lie between 1520 and 1523. The play was published as a *suelta* ("loose fascicule") during the interval of the two editions of the *Propalladia*, that is, between 1517 and 1524, and was included in the 1524 edition of the *Propalladia* (Naples).[1] A printer's corrector, Hernando Merino, composed a poem as a preface to the *suelta* that may be interpreted to imply that Torres Naharro may already have been dead.[2] As was noted in Chapter 1, Gillet surmises that Torres Naharro may have died by 1531 and perhaps as early as 1520. But this is only speculation, logical though it may seem, and all one can really say is that the *Aquilana* was printed as an undated *suelta* before 1524. After its addition to the *Propalladia* of 1524, the play appeared also in the Seville edition of his works in 1526.[3] It remains as the last known dramatic work by Torres Naharro. It is the longest, with 3114 lines,[4] and as such, serves as a compendium of the author's ideas.

Gillet agreed that this was a romantic comedy, but for Green the play is "half romantic comedy and half *Gelegenheitsstück*" (IV, 545). Green probably meant that this romantic comedy was used as a play of occasion. One category does not exclude the other, but rather, the two overlap with a simultaneously functional purpose. In part, the drama parodies the styles of courtly love. The burlesque is present in that it shows that the woman, Felicina, is as much of a pursuer as is the man, much in the same manner as Melibea seeks Calisto, or as in modern times, George Bernard Shaw's heroine of *Man and Superman* pursues the male. The gallant lover, Aquilano, suffers in ways similar to Calisto's.

Though not as tightly structured as the *Ymenea*, this work is on a par with the *Calamita*, and superior to the *Seraphina*. The *Aquilana* is replete with entertaining devices, although they do not always move the story forward. The piece lacks the emotional, suspenseful tension of the *Ymenea* and the involved plot of the *Calamita*, but stands above them for its lyricism and its philosophical aphorisms.

Both Juan de Valdés and Menéndez y Pelayo criticized the inconsistent linguistic decorum of this play. Although Valdés liked its unaffected style, the language and sometimes the actions of the nobility did not reflect their august position.[5] Some have found this lack of respect for regal decorum repugnant, as did Moratín, but Torres Naharro thereby expressed an antimonarchical sentiment prevalent in his period. Lack of respect for the aristocracy in general as well as for the church hierarchy in particular fostered ridicule and indecorous treatment of leaders and of the institutions that propagated them.

Torres Naharro was fully conscious of what he was doing in this work. He had already essayed fictional comedy with the *Seraphina* and had written the *Ymenea*, a well-structured landmark for the Spanish stage. In the *Aquilana* he was repeating the framework tested in the *Calamita*, with a few technical changes and a slight prolongation of the action, which tended to detract from the tight construction, inasmuch as Torres Naharro had not quite mastered the art of the full-length play like Lope's, Tirso's, Calderón's, or Shakespeare's. The plot of the *Aquilana* likewise resembles that of the *Ymenea* with conversations at the window, the night scenes, and secret rendezvous not only of masters but also of servants. There is, antithetically, a strong difference between the two plays. There is no presence of ominous danger in the *Aquilana* as there is from the beginning of the *Ymenea*. The guardian of family honor (Bermudo) does not loom as a serious threat to the lovers until late in the play. There is no sustained drive for vengeance nor an air of bitter animosity as there is in the *Ymenea*, and no creation of a fever-pitch suspense. Consequently, the *Aquilana* calls for a more sedate, philosophical, and reflective type of performance.

III   *Sources*

As for other plays by Torres Naharro, the sources are numerous, ranging from the popular and oral to the learned and literary. And as in the previous plays, Torres Naharro continues to synthesize, adapt, modify, and vary his source material. The setting itself is an example: the garden scene may come from *La Celestina* which utilizes a variation of the street scene of the Plautine comedy.[6] The garden scene alternates with scenes inside the king's palace. Actually, we have here the same basic type of scene as in the *Ymenea* or *Calamita:* one side of the stage reveals a cross-section of a room. A combination of the two types of scenes—the garden and the house, or the street scene and the house—is one that could arise from the theatrical ingenuity of Torres Naharro. He demonstrates this new approach to the Spanish theater by borrowing effects from the classical Latin comedy, from the humanistic Italian pieces, and from the innovations of *La Celestina*.

Influences from classical comedy can be readily identified. As in

the Latin comedy, the servant is called upon for advice and proceeds to assume charge of Aquilano's situation.[7] Faceto is intricately
involved in his master's case and in the end reveals his master's
identity in order to deliver him from mortal difficulty and thus to
bring the play to a happy conclusion.[8] Torres Naharro also picks up a
variation of the device of anagnorisis. This device, typical of Latin
comedy, was renewed in the humanistic drama. Aquilano, who for
six years has been a squire in Bermudo's court, is disclosed in reality
to be the son of the king of Hungary.[9] Even the Latin terminology of
servus for "slave" is employed by the playwright as *siervo* ("servant"), a term not previously used in the known Spanish drama.

As in the Latin comedy, servants are expected to be discreet.
Contingent on that discretion they can then be esteemed as *her-
manos* ("brothers and sisters") (II, 465, 184; 506, 80). The fraternal
feeling, part and parcel of the Christian and Renaissance outlook,
was integrated into the daily life of the Spaniard. It is significant that
the feeling of brotherhood between master and servant was not
expected to be mutual. Servants did not reciprocate by calling their
masters, or mistresses, "brother" or "sister"; it was rather a mark of
condescension that the master could make to his servant. The
equalizing element was a descending one, but not an ascending one,
brought about by a patronizing attitude toward the servant class.

The request for a reward for good news is a further variation on
the Latin comedy theme of the slave asking either for his freedom or
for a favor in return for good tidings or for specially good deeds.
Grismer writes that "In the *Asinaria* the servant Libanus takes advantage of his master's anxiety to hear the news by forcing the girl
Phalaenium to kiss and make love to him, and by insisting that
Argyrippus get down on all fours and carry him astride his back. The
young lover and his sweetheart suffer these humiliations to learn the
tidings the slave bears them."[10] Torres Naharro adapts this scene to
the final act of *Aquilana* in which Felicina must beseech her servant
Dileta on her knees, kiss her hand, and carry her train in order to
hear the desirable news. This type of turnabout is traceable to the
Roman custom of the Saturnalia, celebrated on December 17. On
that day the slaves and servants of a household were allowed to take
the place of their masters who in turn served and catered to their
commands, with some limitations, no doubt.

The device of eavesdropping may also derive from Plautus' plays.
It appears frequently in *La Celestina* of Rojas[11] and in the farces of

Lucas Fernández, who dealt with it in the *Comedy* where the grandfather Juan Benito overhears part of the courting between Bras Gil and Beringuella. Torres Naharro uses the eavesdropping device in the *Jacinta* and *Calamita* as well as the *Aquilana*. Among other dramatic methods that go back to the Latin comedy, boasting by the cowardly servant is present, while name-calling was transferred to the device of *pullas*. Thus Torres Naharro made capital use of the expertise of the dramatists who had preceded him, a contributing factor to the popularity his plays enjoyed and to their becoming models for later dramatists. Besides the classical drama, instances of classical influence also extend to Ovid's *Metamorphoses*. Italian influences including Castiglione's *Il Cortegiano* were noticed by Green and Gillet, while for the source of the gardeners there is the *Egloga de Breno* (1511) by Salazar.

Torres Naharro was quick to profit by native Spanish fountains of inspiration. Reminiscences of *La Celestina* appear when the servants overhear what goes on between the lovers; similarly, Felicina's thought of suicide for love is a mockery of Melibea's action when she is on the verge of casting herself off a tower.[12] This scene may ultimately regress to Boccaccio's *Fiammetta* which may have inspired Rojas' own treatment of the event in *La Celestina* (III, 807, n. 43).

There are even conceptual parallelisms with *La Celestina*. Felicina, speaking of Aquilano, employs similar terms to those that Melibea uttered with reference to Celestina: "ni me place quando viene,/ ni me duele quando va" ("neither does it please me when he comes, nor does it grieve me when he leaves") (II, 505, 58–59); "ni tu mensaje me ha traydo prouecho ni de tu yda me puede venir daño" ("neither has your message brought me profit nor can harm come to me from your departure") (*La Celestina*, I, 192). Dileta speaks to Felicina as Celestina does to Melibea: "hazes mala fiesta/ en ser auara contigo/ de lo que poco te cuesta" ("you do ill in being stingy with yourself, with what costs you little") (II, 509, 162–64). Celestina says, "¿Por qué no daremos parte de nuestras gracias e personas a los próximos . . .?" ("Why can't we give a part of our graces and persons to those close to us?") (*La Celestina*, I, 177). Correspondences extend to the two rendezvous in *La Celestina* and the *Aquilana* both of which are at night (*La Celestina*, II, 78; *Aquilana*, II, 505, 47). Like Calisto, Aquilano seethes, insane with love. Faceto, like Sempronio, reminds his master that the girl he loves does not deserve him, in spite of her scorn for him. Faceto's insolence goes beyond that of Sempronio, while the latter is moved by greater self-interest which turns him to disloyalty. The conjuration by the gardeners puts one in mind of the conjuration of the devil by Celestina. Gillet finds this particular episode a parody of a hymn, *Pange Lingua* by St. Thomas Aquinas (III, 74, n. 316). The description of Aquilano's illness is one that follows the poetic tradition of the "Definition of Love" (II, 518–20, 415–74), as found in Juan Ruiz's *Libro de buen amor* (1330), in Rodrigo de Cota's *Diálogo entre el amor y un viejo* (1470), and in Lucas Fernández's *Farce* of Prauos (1497–1499).[13]

The source for the scene between Aquilano and King Bermudo depicting the protagonist's resignation to impending death arises from a historical background entailing the grief-stricken events of the Catholic Sovereigns, and their son Prince Don Juan. There are parallel incidents between the scene of the dying prince, Aquilano, in act 4 and the real-life episode of Prince Juan's death in Salamanca, as described by a chronicler of the Catholic monarchs. Another parallel from real life noticed by D. W. McPheeters is the similarity between Felicina's attempts at suicide and the plight of the surviving wife of Prince Juan as recorded by another writer: "The humanist Ramírez de Villaescusa published an imagined lamentation of the young widow, the Princess Margarita, in which she comes to consider the possibility of suicide and the means that she would utilize, the rope, or falling, or the sword. Fortunately, Queen Isabella succeeds in calming her temper in time."[14] Closely tied to this scene are meditations on death derived from the *Couplets* of Jorge Manrique. We have noted earlier that these couplets find persistent echoes in the entire literary corpus of Torres Naharro.

The source for the scene of the parade of women before the malingering prince can be found in various literary works. One is the Latin story "De integro amico."[15] This exact story may be traced back to a biographical form of the tale, as Crawford suggests,[16] to Plutarch's *Lives,* and the chapter on "Demetrius."[17] An oriental tale suggesting a similar treatment in which a "prince's pulse beats violently when his loved one passes by" is listed by Stith Thompson and Jonas Baly.[18] Another probable source for the *Aquilana* may be a folktale current in Evora, Portugal. It "introduces a lovelorn prince in disguise hailing from far-off Hungary" (III, 806, n. 693). In the sixteenth century, Hungary was a distinctly romantic far-off land, particularly appealing to the Spanish people, due in part to its common cause with Spain against Islam. Spaniards were fighting the sect on the sea while Hungarians were struggling against it at the gates of Europe. Even in his first play, *Diálogo del nascimiento,* Torres Naharro thought of Hungary as a distant and dangerous land. Betiseo's wish for punishment of the pirates who robbed him of his wine, it will be remembered, was that they be sent to Hungary without anything to drink.

Now, looking in the other direction, with respect to parallels of Torres Naharro's plays and those that followed him, it is possible that some influence from Torres Naharro may have filtered to Gil Vicente's *Comedia del viudo* and to *Dom Duardos*.[19] Moreover, the romantic nature of the play and the structure revolving around disguises and confidential servants, along with the five-act division, show an affinity, distant though it be, with some of the effects to be found in Shakespeare's *The Taming of the Shrew.*

IV   *Structure*

Worthy of attention are the foreshadowings, the recapitulations, and the symmetry of the acts, along with the characterization and comedy of the play, which Torres Naharro develops with a formulaic rigidity. In the expository introit, the rustic claims to be sent by the author as his ambassador to his public, and as in the *Ymenea,* his coarse comments are suitable for the ritual of fertility that this wedding play expounds. The plot begins to develop when master and servant go over a letter which provides a basic backdrop as in the *Calamita,* establishing the love interest between Aquilano and Felicina, and indicating that Faceto will parody his master. A broad but false prefiguration of tragic consequences is Aquilano's claim that he will die in his conquest of Felicina (II, 478, 297). His premonition of tragedy casts doubt upon the veracity of the play's title, which asserts that this is a comedy. False prefiguration is seen also in both the *Ymenea* and the *Calamita.*

In the structural pattern, the second act is that of the servants, coming at approximately the same point as the act of the servants in the *Ymenea,* that is some eight hundred lines into the play (869 for the *Ymenea* and 819 for the *Aquilana*), which reveals a deliberately developing plan in Torres Naharro. Besides the engaging humor of the gardeners in this act, the story advances by precipitating the lovers' meeting in the garden.

The theme of love and death is restated by Felicina (II, 504, 24) in act 3. Felicina's pining for her lover is a slight deviation from the pattern of courtly love in which the lady is supposed to be above and beyond such emotion.[20] The element of honor is worked into the plot by involving the king, guardian of the virtue of his daughter and of her royal lineage. Aquilano's noble origin must be disclosed to avert the tragedy, but during the revelation, the author teases his audience. News of such magnitude has to be introduced piecemeal. So Torres Naharro injects a delaying element—in order to prolong the divulging of the secret. The dramatist operates in this teasing manner likewise in the *Calamita*, and again in the final act when Dileta toys with Felicina in retelling her the great secret. Suspense at the end of act 4 in the *Aquilana* is not as intense as that found in the *Ymenea*, but is present when the characters go in search of Felicina, hopefully to reach her before she commits suicide. There are two times when tragic outcomes are pending in this story: the first danger is present when Aquilano's life hangs in the balance, and the second arises when Felicina plans her own death.

Technically, the fourth act leads skillfully into the last, which begins with the appearance of Felicina bent upon committing suicide. For the rest of the play these intentions must be thwarted, and they are. Happiness and harmony become the key words of the denouement, as the marriage of the lovers is announced for the next day. Torres Naharro writes no song for the end of this drama.

A sense of cohesion is developed in the presentation by both foreshadowings and recapitulations. The former are found in long-range and short-range types. Short-range foreshadowing is seen particularly in the final act dealing with Felicina's attempted suicide, when Dileta implies that she will encounter hindrances. In the same act, Dileta enters to request gifts because she has good news; these also foreshadow the happy ending. Appropriately, the last act concentrates on the catastrophe, the unwinding and ordering of the action, and the establishment of a new status quo. Besides prefiguration, the other important device in the structuring of this dramatic presentation is recapitulation. There is greater awareness of it in Torres Naharro than in the earlier Spanish playwrights. Understandably, the structure of modern drama was becoming more clearly defined. Early in the first act it is established that Aquilano is in love with Felicina, but he repeats this fact, "soy tu siervo Aquilano" ("it is your servant, Aquilano") (II, 484, 474), before the act ends. In the second act the relationships of the main characters and the central preoccupation of the lovers is reiterated in a dialogue between Faceto and Dileta. After the intervening humor of the second act and the recapitulation of the third act, the plot is ready once again to deepen with complications in the fourth act. Recapitulation becomes increasingly important as the play mounts to its climax in the fifth act, in order that the audience have the facts clearly in mind for the comprehension of the approaching crucial action that will lead to a new order of lasting relationships.

In the last act what amounts to a recapitulation for the audience, serves as a fresh disclosure for Felicina. Hence, dramatic irony enters to make the climax more impressive. The conscious artistry of Torres Naharro is evident in the various organizational techniques, an ordering which extends to the symmetrical balancing of the speakers, as in the *Calamita*. The neat symmetry continues unabated until the final moments, as for the *Calamita*, when the scenic symmetry gradually falters and the activity is accentuated by the gathering of all the play's participants, now beaming with delight. They remain onstage to tie up the loose ends of the plot and place their world on an orderly path once more. This play is structured without any final song. As a matter of fact music is lacking throughout the performance. On the other hand, there may very well have been music and dancing by the general public attending the wedding feast at the conclusion of the play and detached from its presentation.

The versification is limited to the *coplas de pie quebrado* with the five-line stanza, the short line being the first of the strophe. Thus the short line consists of four syllables, while the other lines are octosyllabic with the rhyme *a a b a b*. And finally, a comment on the language: the dialogues are at times a bit prolix with an accumulation of parallelisms and synonyms, notably in the conjuration of the gardeners and in the confessions of love by the enamored protagonists. Torres Naharro expands the speeches with some redundant superfluities, witness Felicina's harangue against men and Aquilano's diatribe against love. This may very well be in keeping with the comic spirit and burlesque nature of the entire play.

V *The Cast*

Limitations of space do not permit us to go into detail concerning characterization, comedy, and themes, interesting though they be; consequently, we must content ourselves with just brief mentions of some major points. Among ten characters in the play, the males predominate; they number eight, the women are two. The characters include the essentials of the cast of many a Golden Age drama: the gallant and his lady and their respective confidential servants. The last two are exceptionally well delineated in this play. Torres Naharro had by now found a formula upon which he could capitalize with success. It is generally conceded that Torres Naharro excels in the depiction of the popular types vis-á-vis the aristocratic. The reason for this, as Valdés observed, is that Torres Naharro lived among the common people and knew them exceptionally well.

By the time Torres Naharro writes the *Aquilana,* he has begun to type his own characters. He recognized that he had formulated a good plan and took advantage of it. Basically he uses the same kind of situation he had put together with so much success in the *Ymenea* and the *Calamita.* The problem is centered around the difficulties lovers experience when it seems that their love is an impossible one. They encounter enormous, seemingly insurmountable, obstacles to its satisfaction. An outside force or forces complicate matters for the leading man and his lady. In this case that outside force is a parent—the father of the damsel—the protector of the family's honor. Ancillary to the plot are adjunct characters whose purpose is to prolong the play with additional complexities and even with seemingly irrelevant moments of comic relief. These sideline characters that come and go in the *Aquilana* as the dramatist dictates, are the rustic gardeners (descendants of Encina's and Fernández's shepherds) and the learned physicians.

The charactonyms play a fundamental part in establishing the personality of each player. The name Aquilano can signify the nature and likeness of an eagle, a symbol of majesty, royalty, a sovereign lover. Furthermore, the Latin root *aquilus* means "hidden." Thus Aquilano, a courtly lover, functions as a binary symbol for royalty and for the protagonist's hidden identity. Felicina suggests *felicidad* ("happiness"). She is first amusing, then firm, and later a caricature of a forsaken woman. When her fortune turns, she represents the ultimate happiness for all. Faceto (witty, humorous) is amusing, as his Italian name states, and as it is translated into the Spanish, a *gracioso.* Similarly, Dileta is a reflection of her name (Italian, *diletta,* "delightful"). She and Faceto are catalysts to the action. Bermudo was actually the name of a king of León, not of Castile, and this bit of unreality adds to the setting of the *comedia a fantasía*. The comical gardeners' names, Dandario and Galterio, provide little information except that the latter's name is of a Germanic background. The doctors' names, of familiar classical origin, are more meaningful. The three physicians' descend from established, legendary figures, and Torres Naharro uses them for typecasting and dramatic economy. Esculapio was a legendary Greek god of medicine and Podalirio, or Polidario with metathesis, one of his two sons. Galieno was a distinguished Greek physician, founder of physiology (III, 714, n. 238).

What role does Torres Naharro choose for himself in this play? Conceivably, the dramatist played the key role of Faceto, who acts for the author, confidently concluding the play and addressing the audience as a director would. This is in keeping with Torres Naharro's accustomed role as director of entertainments.

VI *Coalescing of the* Gracioso

Torres Naharro uses a myriad of methods to achieve comedy. Throughout the play there are asides, jokes, and flippant remarks intended to induce merriment. But it is the perfection of the leading man's comic sidekick that is the significant innovation in this play. Faceto is the realization of the elements distributed in Turpedio, Boreas, and Lenicio, a figure that is assuming a prominent dramatic role. He is already described in this play as the *gracioso*. Dileta says of him, "¡O gratioso!/ Nunca te vi tan donoso,/ ni en tus hablas tan galán ("O witty one! I never saw you so clever, nor so gallant in your speech") (II, 501, 410–12). The term *gracioso* as applied here takes a long time in being incorporated into the precepts of the dramatists. We find the figure officially mentioned in them only in the seventeenth century when Ricardo de Turia writes (in 1616) that the comic poets produce humor by introducing "en las comedias un lacayo que en son de gracioso" ("in the plays a lackey who in the manner of a *gracioso*") is not removed from any secrets of the most genteel lady nor of the queen, but even the most profound secrets of love and state are open to him.[21] This is true. Although Lope de Vega in his *Arte nuevo de hacer comedias* (1609) does not single out the *gracioso* for comment, surely the term had long since been freely applied to this ubiquitous character of his theater.

VII   *Themes and Ideas*

Torres Naharro's last play was a compendium of his ideas as well as a further concretization of his theatrical formula. His art, like any other, attempts to create an alternate reality, an improvement over the harsh facts of life. He therefore develops philosophical and social ideas vented through the dialogue. In their multiple purposes one of the gardeners' functions in akin to the shepherds of the liturgical Christmas play. They are characterized by an underlying current of didacticism, because the torn teacher in Torres Naharro can not be suppressed. The honor theme is coupled with love in this play as it is in the two preceding ones. In the *Ymenea,* a brother is charged with its preservation, in the *Calamita* and the *Aquilana* it is the father who is its guardian.

Along with honor and personal merit, a rebelious democratic sentiment is a major concern of the several social classes represented in the play. Reasonable men had never let any one sector of a society monopolize honor, and during the Renaissance, honor had ceased even more definitely to be thought of as the exclusive prerogative of the nobility. In fact, those who held power were being discredited. During the years leading to the Reformation an office like that of a cleric, or even of a pope and a king, had lost its temporal luster. It was no longer unthinkable to permit honor to exist beyond the ken and merit of the upper classes. In fact, its existence among the latter was questioned. Those who had held religious office had too often debased their occupation, so that it became stripped of any semblance of dignity that would have made it worthy of admiration. Hence the gardener could satirize the wayward cleric and equally downgrade the office of the king (II, 490, 89; 491, 123–24).

Along with honor, faith, the idea of democracy, and personal freedom of choice, love is the strongest theme of the drama. It attacks the young, spares the old, but baffles all. Love like truth prevails above everything else. Unity and harmony are ultimately established when love, life's indispensable ingredient, is allowed free expression. Yet, there is one restriction for Torres Naharro. Reciprocated love can best flourish among members of the same social stratum, a lesson found in Torres Naharro's last three *comedias a fantasia*. Love may begin on different levels, but by means of anagnorisis it is discovered that love has endured only by the attraction of equals. Torres Naharro sounds a hesitant note of change from the old aristocratic life of order to the renewed order of personal dignity. A thread of individual worth flows through this play suggesting, at least remotely, that one can possibly obtain a spouse beyond his social level provided his personal merits are strong enough to overcome the drawbacks of a humble background.

The general air of insubordination in the play is used primarily for dramatic purposes. Nevertheless, it expresses Torres Naharro's ideas. The upsurge of democratic feeling was manifest everywhere and particularly in the works of the dramatists who voiced the popular sentiments during the era of transition leading to the Reformation. The periodic generational disrespect for governing circles is a typical facet of a social upheaval. Torres Naharro was gravely disillusioned by the callousness of members of the ruling aristocracy, and was instrumental in stripping them of their hypocritical masks.

The structural and thematic sophistication of the *Aquilana* serves as a reminder of the indebtedness the Golden Age dramatists owed to their forerunners. The dramatic seeds sown by the early dramatists like Encina and Fernández budded in the work of Torres Naharro and blossomed in the schools of Lope de Vega, Tirso de Molina, and Calderón de la Barca. Although Torres Naharro was "primitive" in the temporal sense of the word, his talents were far in advance for the youthful period of the Spanish theater which savored the excitement of his gifted work.

acts from five to four, then to three; yet a hundred years after Torres Naharro, the five-act division was still adhered to successfully by no less a figure than Shakespeare.

It is difficult in one work to treat exhaustively of Torres Naharro's fine artistic methods. In the preceding chapters we have attempted to trace the sources, characteristics, and the impact of his works. Though he essayed gamely, but without distinction, into briefer poetic compositions, his remarkable creative forte remained the dramatic form. In the *comedia a noticia*, the documentary play, he entered the plotless harshness of life's chaotic patterns, while in the fictional play, the *comedia a fantasía*, he let the world of make-believe reign supreme. While the playwright allowed anguish and passions to complicate life, in the end these were submitted to the control of idealized reason. The *comedia a noticia* lacks plot structure, whereas the *comedia a fantasía*, based on metaphorical representation of reality, contains a clearly discernible plot, and a unity of action that builds to a climax and tapers off to a predetermined conclusion. The chaos of life gives way to poetic harmony and thus leads to a universally sought tranquillity that is best granted by the magic of art.

Torres Naharro was therefore not only a structural precursor of the baroque drama, but also its thematic contributor, emphasizing love, honor, free will and social justice. His literary work can be interpreted in part as a depiction of personalized history—history on an individual microcosmic level, in juxtaposition to the macrocosmic level of history revealed by political events. Through his art his own world view is a reflection not only of his immediate audience but also of the changing society about him. While Torres Naharro explores the themes of the human condition, man interplaying with society, he rises on occasion to the philosophical plane, revising traditional attitudes and in a subtle way shifting them to the fantasy world of poetic existence.

Not all his art was devoted to the development of new structural and aesthetic guides for the theater. He expressed his cherished thoughts for a more humane world, propagating his ideas for socioeconomic equality. His fearless criticism of prevalent social abuses before the variegated audience attracted the collective minds of his countrymen for whom his art served as a vehicle for expressing their own aspirations. Through his artistic inventiveness there surged emotions against the unjust treatment of his fellowman. At times Torres Naharro seemed to resent the unmerited wealth of those holding high positions and exercising abusive selfish power. But he was capable of transcending these feelings of resentment. In a world of limited spheres of action, he sensed the common denominator of his spectators to be the longing to eliminate injustice and to instigate freedom of expression for the irrepressible human will.

In the course of our study we have seen the innovations and influences that the individual plays contributed to the evolving and expanding scope of the Spanish theater. There is no noticeable linear progression toward perfection of Torres Naharro's art; he reached that stage of perfection at the time he composed his masterpiece, the *Comedia Ymenea,* but once he had developed his formula, he moved toward variations of that formula. Such variations did not stop with him, but were fostered, propelled, and perpetuated through many successful adaptations by the generations of playwrights that followed him.

Notes and References

Preface

1. All textual translations, except where otherwise indicated, are by John Lihani.

2. There seems to be a phrase missing at this point which would state that the breaks between the "journeys" constitute the intermissions or resting places, rather than implying that the "journeys" themselves are the resting places, as this context does.

3. Torres Naharro uses Castilian in the sense of "Spanish." In his works he also presents Latin and Valencian terms as well as other dialects and languages.

Chapter One

1. *Propalladia and Other Works of Bartolomé de Torres Naharro*, ed. Joseph E. Gillet, 4 vols. (Bryn Mawr: University of Pennsylvania Press, 1943–1961, (Volume 4 was transcribed, edited, and completed by Otis H. Green). In volume 4 p. 402, Gillet opts for the latter date (1485), deducing it from what Jacinto says in the *Comedia Jacinta* (1515). The play's protagonist states that he is then thirty years old. Gillet feels that is a reflection of Torres Naharro's age. On the other hand, R. E. Chandler and K. Schwartz, in *A New History of Spanish Literature* ([Louisiana State University Press, 1961], p. 73), give the year of Torres Naharro's birth as 1476. This would make him only two years younger than Lucas Fernández, and eight years younger than Juan del Encina, two other coetaneous Spanish dramatists of the early Salamancan school.

Henceforth, references to Gillet's edition of the *Propalladia* will be cited in the text; in these references a Roman numeral represents the volume, followed by the page (in Arabic) and, when necessary, a line number.

2. Several leads on similar names have been followed up in efforts to cast new light on Torres Naharro's life, but to date without substantial results. The most promising lead seems to have been that of the theologian, Bartolomé de Torres (b. 1485?–1512?; d. 1568) who was apparently born in

the province of Burgos and died in the Canary Islands. This eminent prelate is worthy of a separate study, but due to space restrictions we can not go into it here. Yet another approach for seeking additional information on Torres Naharro is to scrutinize the possibility that Medina de las Torres rather than Torre de Miguel Sesmero may have been his birthplace.

3. J. López Prudencio, "Los Naharros de la Torre de Miguel Sesmero," *Revista del Centro de Estudios Extremeños* 1 (1934), 163. A society named in honor of the playwright continues to exist in Torre de Miguel Sesmero, its members hoping someday to discover more information on him.

4. Menéndez y Pelayo also suggests that Torres Naharro and Juan del Encina knew each other in Salamanca. Menéndez y Pelayo quotes a passage from Encina in which he suspects that a Bartolomé named in the poem is Torres Naharro: "¡Para el cuerpo de sant Polo/ Que estoy asmado de ti!/ ¿Quién te arribó por aquí/ Tan lagrimoso y tan solo?/ Yo cuidé qu'eras Bartolo,/ Un pastor de Extremadura/ Que aprisca en aquel altura" ("By the body of St. Paul, I'm surprised at you! Who brought you here so tearful and alone? I thought you were Bartolo, a shepherd from Extremadura who herds his sheep at those heights") (M. Menéndez y Pelayo, *Estudios de crítica literaria*, vol. 3 [Madrid: Hijos de Tello, 1920], 15). This very same name appears in Encina's *Égloga de Plácida y Vitoriano* (performed in Italy in 1513) wherein Bartolo is a cleric. It would suggest that Encina and Torres Naharro knew each other in Rome as well as in Spain. We know that in 1513 Torres Naharro was in Italy and may have become ordained by then, thus making it possible for him to serve the Spanish colony there as a priest as well as one of its entertainers. If he was not yet ordained, he could have been serving as a lay priest for a determined period. The passage that could be enlightening in future research appears as: "Demos prissa,/ antes que diga missa/ el nuestro crego Bartolo" ("Let's hurry up, before the mass is said by our cleric Bartolo") (J. del Encina, *Églogas*, ed. H. López Morales [Madrid: Escelicer, 1963], p. 308).

5. It is quite possible that Fernando de Rojas before writing *La Celestina* may have belonged to this thespian group while a student at Salamanca. Stephen Gilman seems tempted to draw a relationship between Torres Naharro and Rojas, apparently suspecting that Bartolomé de Torres Naharro was brother-in-law of Alonso de Montalbán, who was father-in-law of Fernando de Rojas. (See Gilman, *The Spain of Fernando de Rojas* [Princeton, 1972], p. 557.) In a recent personal note, Gilman has withdrawn support for this relationship, and considers the statement an error of the compiler of the index for his book.

6. From Extremadura came such men as Hernando Cortés, the conqueror of Mexico, and Francisco Pizarro, conqueror of Peru, both of whom were of the same adventurous generation as Torres Naharro.

7. John Lihani, "New Biographical Ideas on Bartolomé de Torres

Naharro," *Hispania* 54 (1971), 828–35. In the *Addición del diálogo,* the rustic Herrando professes to be a *medio escolar* ("half scholar"), much like the *medio gramata* ("half literate") shepherd of the introit. Herrando is referred to as *Hi del moro* ("Son of a Moor") (IV, 288, 200), and this epithet fits with the other knowledge we have of Torres Naharro's family background. Both characters could reflect the life of the playwright. The suggestion here that Herrando, played by Torres Naharro, has a Moorish connection is reinforced by Herrando's concentration on Moorish curses as his comment in his satire of church officers indicates, "le salte al beneficiado vn asno morisco" ("may a Moorish donkey jump out on him [the curate]") (I, 289, 245). Moorish themes, close to the heart of Torres Naharro, may be a further reflection of Moorish background.

8. In the *Diálogo del nascimiento,* in his travels, Betiseo went overland from Santiago to Rome. It took him three months to get to Lyons, France, and two more months to reach Rome. At this point, in the vicinity of Rome, he was accosted by thieves, perhaps coast raiding pirates, held up and searched by them, stripped, and his wine flask emptied. Betiseo, expressing Torres Naharro's personal experiences, would thus sing glowing nostalgic words about Spain, and mirror Torres Naharro's initial dislike of Italy, considering it "d' españoles sepoltura" ("a tomb for Spaniards") (I, 194). Stanislav Zimic rejects the idea that Betiseo represents Torres Naharro ("El pensamiento humanístico y satírico de Torres Naharro," *Boletín de la Biblioteca Menéndez y Pelayo,* 52 (1976), 23.)

9. J. Lohse, *Vittoria Colonna* (Florence: Giannini & Son, 1912).

10. In note 4 we have already noted a possible reference to him. Though Gillet (IV, 409) feels it was not likely that Torres Naharro associated with Italian artists or writers of his time, there can be no doubt that he knew some of them.

11. Gillet (IV, 405), and in *Propalladia,* ed. M. Menéndez y Pelayo (Madrid: Real Academia Española, 1900), II, xii.

12. The Gonzaga archives in Mantua contain a letter by Isabella d'Este, dated December 8, 1514, and sent from Naples, in which she speaks to her secretary, Benedetto Capilupi, of a Spanish play that she had seen the day before. It could have been performed by someone like Torres Naharro. For further reference to this letter please see note 3 to chapter seven.

13. M. Menéndez y Pelayo, ed., *Propalladia,* II, lxvi, n. 2.

14. Bartolomé de Torres, the theologian (1512?–1568), is the author of a work first published in 1566 and republished after his death, *Commentaria in 17 Questiones primae partis S. Thomae de Aquino de ineffabili trinitatis mysterio* (Venice: Juntal, 1588). This prelate was buried in the Cathedral of Las Palmas, Canary Islands. (See, Beltrán de Heredia, "La facultad de teología en la Universidad de Sigüenza," *Revista española de teología* 3 [1943], 438.)

Chapter Two

1. See O. H. Green, *Spain and the Western Tradition* (Madison: University of Wisconsin Press, 1968), II, 280–81, 319.

2. Fernando Francisco de Ávalos was born in Italy, but of Spanish descent. He was put in command of Spanish troops in Italy.

3. For a study of Torres Naharro's versification in his drama, see S. G. Morley, "Strophes in the Spanish Drama before Lope de Vega," in *Homenaje a Menéndez Pidal* (Madrid: Hernando, 1925), I, 510–31.

4. *Comedia Jacinta* (II, 330, 5–12), in *Comedia Ymenea* (II, 278, 7–12; 314, 109–56); *Comedia Aquilana* (II, 494, 195–224); *Comedia Calamita* (II, 438, 1–28): and the *Comedia Seraphina* (II, 50, 420–520).

Chapter Three

1. Gillet writes, "A popular variety of *pulla* is an anecdote which elicits easy rhyme words or indecent rejoinder or malediction" (*Prop.*, IV, 43). J. P. W. Crawford has commented on "Echarse pullas," in *Romanic Review* 6 (1915), 150–64. Meredith adds that the *pullas* "consisted of a contest in which one person wished all sorts of misfortunes, for the most part obscene, upon another who replied in a similar strain" (J. A. Meredith, *Introito and Loa in the Drama of the Sixteenth Century* [Philadelphia: University of Pennsylvania, 1928], pp. 40–41.) The *pullas* are a typical form of insult, a show of hostility expressed in exaggerated form to make listeners laugh and to throw the target of the remarks off balance. The object is to make the adversary lose self-control—he who loses control, loses the contest. *Pullas* were a popular adjunct to the comic effects. The repertory for *pullas* was abundant enough to have them cataloged alphabetically according to the profession or social aspects being satirized (*Prop.*, IV, 42).

2. The idea for the introit may germinate in the initial pronouncements by the shepherd of the farces of Lucas Fernández, while the argument is handed down from the Latin dramatists. John Lihani, *Lucas Fernández* (New York: Twayne, 1973), p. 141, and Meredith, *Introito and Loa in the Spanish Drama*.

3. John Lihani, "Lucas Fernández and the Evolution of the Shepherd's Family Pride in Early Spanish Drama," *Hispanic Review* 25 (1957), 252–63.

4. The observations made by Marcelino Menéndez y Pelayo, *Estudios de crítica literaria*, pp. 111–17, and the contributions by Gillet with the modifications to these by Green (*Prop.*, IV, 550–62) are considered to be the most important for an orientation on the drama of Torres Naharro.

5. See Lihani, *Lucas Fernández*, pp. 118–30.

6. Sayagués is a dialect of Sayago, a town in León of western Spain. The term became a catchall for dialectal Spanish when found in the speech of the rustics of the Spanish theater. Originally, the dialect used in the theatrical performances was the *charro* of Salamanca, found in the works of Lucas

Fernández and his contemporaries, including Encina and, of course, Torres Naharro. See John Lihani, *El lenguaje de Lucas Fernández: estudio del dialecto sayagués* (Bogotá: Instituto Caro y Cuervo, 1973), pp. 3–8.

7. M. Menéndez y Pelayo, *Estudios*, p. 113.

Chapter Four

1. Ilis longest play is the *Aquilana*, published in the 1524 edition of the *Propalladia*.

2. J. P. W. Crawford, *Spanish Drama before Lope de Vega* (Philadelphia: University of Pennsylvania, 1937), pp. 91–93.

3. The Valencian portions of the play have been studied by H. Corbato, "El Valenciano en la *Propalladia* de Torres Naharro," *Romance Philology* 3 (1950), 262–70.

4. M. Menéndez y Pelayo, *Estudios*, p. cxx, and M. Romera-Navarro, "Estudio de la *Comedia Himenea* de Torres Naharro," *Romanic Review* 12 (1921), 60.

5. See examples in D. Radcliff Umstead's *The Birth of Modern Comedy in Renaissance Italy* (Chicago: University of Chicago Press, 1969), pp. 246–76.

6. This conceit keeps reappearing, and, in an exceptionally notable way, in San Juan de la Cruz's "Coplas del alma que pena por ver a Dios" ("Couplets of the Soul that Yearns to See God"), in *The Penguin Book of Spanish Verse*, ed. J. M. Cohen, rev. ed. (Baltimore: Penguin Books, 1960), p. 182, and in Santa Teresa de Jesús' gloss of *Las Moradas*, in *Biblioteca de autores españoles*, vol. 53, pp. 509–510.

7. S. G. Morley, *Spanish Ballads* (New York: Holt, 1911), p. 64. For further treatment of these sources as well as references to others, see Gillet, IV, 486–87.

8. Juan de Valdés, *Diálogo de la lengua* (Madrid: Clás. cast., 1953), p. 164; and N. D. Shergold, *History of the Spanish Stage* (Oxford: Clarendon Press, 1967), p. 152; C. de Villalón, *Ingeniosa comparación entre lo antiguo y lo presente*, ed. M. Serrano y Sanz (Madrid: Soc. de bibl. esp., 1898).

Chapter Five

1. Leandro Fernández de Moratín, *Orígenes del teatro español* (Madrid, 1944), II, 185.

2. M. Menéndez y Pelayo, *Historia de las ideas estéticas en España* (Madrid, 1946–1947), p. cvii, and *Prop.*, IV, 509.

3. Correas explained that the name Guzmán has a special significance, "Es de los godos; es de los Guzmanes: Cuando uno presume de muy honrado linaje; porque los españoles en común se precian de venir de los godos, y los Guzmanes son linaje noble, y muchos" ("He is of the Goths; he is of the Guzmanes; when one presumes to be of a very honored lineage; because

generally the Spaniards pride themselves of coming from Goths, and the Guzmanes are a very noble lineage") (Gonzalo Correas, *Vocabulario de refranes y frases proverbiales* [Madrid: Revista de archivos, bibliotecas y museos, 1924], p. 574).

In this regard Gillet quotes Diego Montes, *Instrucción y regimiento de guerra* (Çaragoça, 1537, ap. Gallardo, *Ensayo*, III, 858f.), as saying of the Guzmanes, "Estos tales andan siempre muy aderezados y galanes: traen muy lucidas armas: huélganse de hacer cosas señaladas porque sean conocidos" ("Such as these go around well decked out and gallant: they have very showy weapons: they are happy to do significant things so that they be recognized"). Gillet adds, "Later however, their record deteriorated, for in the third quarter of the [sixteenth] century *Guzmán* had become a synonym for *soldado fanfarrón* [boastful soldier] and *cobarde* [coward]" *Prop.*, III, 411, n. 199ff.). Torres Naharro's view comes through Guzmán, feels Gillet, "which shows evidence of the long medieval tradition, yet also the spirit of the Renaissance because the embodiment of liberality is here neither God nor the king nor the nobleman, but an adventurer" (*Prop.*, IV, 250). But one wonders whether Guzmán really was the embodiment of liberality. He schemed for his own profit at the expense of others.

4. Lucas Fernández, *Farsas y églogas*, ed. John Lihani (New York: Las Americas, 1969), pp. 107–10.

5. Eugen Kohler, *Representaciones de Juan del Encina* (Strasbourg: Heitz & Mündel, n.d.), p. 142.

6. F. Vindel, *El arte tipográfico en España durante el siglo XV* (Madrid: Dir. General de Relaciones Culturales, 1951).

Chapter Six

1. Whitaker's Almanac (London: Whitaker, 1976), p. 188.

2. The interlocutor of the prologue clarifies the situation of the show calling it first a *juego* ("play") (II, 83, 7) and then the usual term *comedia* ("comedy") (II, 89, 213, 217). It is finally referred to toward the end of the performance as a *fiesta* (II, 129, 4).

3. Prince João was the object of many such recitations of the virtues of a Christian prince. To celebrate him as an infant, Gil Vicente burst into the chamber of the prince's mother, Queen María, and sang his congratulations to the parents with praises and prognostications in the *Herdsman's Monologue* (1502). Following Gil's monologue came a procession of thirty companions that presented gifts to the newborn king-to-be (J. H. Parker, *Gil Vicente*, [New York: Twayne], p. 30).

4. "Es un diálogo insìpido, dilatado con episodios impertinentes, inconsecuencias y chocarrerías" (M. Menéndez y Pelayo, *Estudios de crítica literaria* [Madrid: Hijos de Tello, 1920], p. 34).

5. "No le des tú essa palmada,/ ves aquí,/ ni l'as de hazer ansí,/ ni tú no t'as de reir" ("Don't give him that slap on the back, see here; nor are you to do thus, nor should you laugh") (II, 109, 245–48).

6. Lihani, *El lenguaje de Lucas Fernández,* p. 35.
7. A discussion of classification problems is found in Nora Weinerth, "The Experimental Theatre of Bartolomé de Torres Naharro," (Ph.D. diss., Harvard University, 1976).
8. Gillet erroneously places the Latin play before Sannazaro's (*Prop.,* IV, 498).
9. Parker, *Gil Vicente,* p. 48.
10. "These were the verses sung or recited by young Apollo in his triumphal chariot, and of which he then handed over written copies to Fama, who, at his request distributed or scattered them over the room" (*Prop.,* III, 324, n. 291).
11. Charlotte Stern, "The Early Spanish Drama: from Medieval Ritual to Renaissance Art," *Renaissance Drama* 6 (1973), 195.

Chapter Seven

1. Considerable information is provided on this Renaissance woman in J. Lohse, *Vittoria Colonna.*
2. J. P. W. Crawford, "Two Notes on the Plays of Torres Naharro," *Hispanic Review* 5 (1937); 76–77.
3. "Yesterday morning I was invited by the Count of Claramonte . . . . After we got up from the table, the women began to dance two by two in their way, and then even man and woman together. Thus the dance lasted two or three hours. After the dance, a certain farce was performed in the Spanish manner which was quite nice. It lasted about an hour and a half . . . ." I am indebted to my colleague, Professor William F. Prizer of the University of Kentucky for directing my attention to this document. It is found in Archivio di Stato di Mantova, Archivio Gonzaga, Copialettere di Isabella d' Este, Envelope 2996, bk. 31, fols. 56v–57v.
4. Stephen Gilman, "Retratos de conversos en la *Comedia Jacinta* de Torres Naharro," *Nueva revista de filología hispánica* 17 (1963–1964), 38.
5. Gilman, *The Spain of Fernando de Rojas,* p. 457.
6. Ibid. The custom of stopping travelers to gather news reports was found even among the ancient Gauls. See, M. Menéndez y Pelayo, *Estudios de crítica literaria* (Madrid, 1920), p. 151.
7. Gilman sees in the three "a cast of fugitive *conversos* barely concealed under flimsy pastoral disguise" (Gilman, *The Spain of Fernando de Rojas,* p. 24, n. 26).
8. This can be compared to the *medio studiante* ("half student") sobriquet for Caxcoluzio of the *Trophea* (II, 88, 185).
9. Gillet prefers to identify Jacinto with Torres Naharro (IV, 113, 250, 384, 521), even when he erroneously, perhaps subconsciously, attributes one of Jacinto's speeches to Pagano (IV, 160, 384, 395, 408).
10. "qu's con ellos el viuir/ mucho peor que la muerte" (II, 363, 247–48). Compare Areúsa's declaration, "he quesido más viuir en mi pequeña casa, esenta e señora, que no en sus ricos palacios sojuzgada e catiua" ("I've

preferred to live in my little house, free and a mistress, rather than in their rich palaces, subjugated and a captive") (*La Celestina*, II, 43).

11. "La filosofía consoladora y optimista constituye el principal mérito de la *Comedia Jacinta*" (M. Menéndez y Pelayo, *Estudios*, p. 117).

Chapter Eight

1. M. Menéndez y Pelayo, *Estudios de crítica literaria* (Madrid: Hijos de Tello, 1920), III, 130.

2. Carvajal was named cardinal in 1493, and died in Rome in 1522 (*Prop.*, III, 413, n. 219).

3. Gillet states that the play has 2763 lines, an obvious misreading of a 7 for a 4 (*Prop.*, III, 459, n. 111).

4. The *Tinellaria* is named after a place, the servants' dining room. The name of the *Soldadesca* comes from its theme, the life of a soldier; and *Trophea* is about an event, to show the triumphal trophies of the Portuguese conquests in Africa and the East. Others like the *Aquilana*, *Ymenea*, *Jacinta*, and *Calamita* are named after the protagonist.

5. Barrabás' preparation for the supper at Lucrecia's house reminds one of the supper at Celestina's house, where the food was supplied by the servant's stealing from the master's kitchen.

6. "jamás en nuestra castellana lengua visto ni oydo" ("never before seen or heard in our Castilian language") (Fernando de Rojas, *La Celestina*, ed. J. Cejádor y Frauca [Madrid: Clás. cast., 1931], I, 5).

7. Compare: "la grandeza del mar es igual al pequeño como al grande" ("the greatness of the sea is equal to the small and to the great") (II, 190, 26–29), with the famous strophe from Jorge Manrique's *Coplas*: "Nuestras vidas son los ríos/ que van a dar en la mar,/ que es el morir./ Allí van los señoríos/ derechos a se acabar/ y consumir;/ allí los ríos caudales,/ allí los otros, medianos,/ y más chicos:/ allegados son iguales/ los que viven por sus manos/ y los ricos" ("Our lives are like the rivers that flow to the sea, which is death. There go the lordships directly to end and be consumed; there the big rivers, there the other medium ones, and smaller, and upon arriving all are equal, those who live by their hands, and the wealthy"). This evokes the verse from Eccles. 1:7: "All the rivers run into the sea;/ yet the sea is not full; unto the place from whence the rivers come, thither they return again."

8. *La vida de Lazarillo de Tormes*, ed. J. Cejador y Frauca (Madrid: Clás. cast., 1941), p. 177.

9. "Pensando ganar, murió/ mi padre, yendo a la guerra" ("Thinking to make a gain, my father died, going off to war") (II, 223, 443–44). Compare with "se hizo cierta armada . . . fue mi padre . . . fenesció su vida" ("an armada was organized . . . my father went . . . he ended his life") (*Lazarillo de Tormes*, ed. Cejador y Frauca, pp. 67–68).

10. Ibid., p. 102. The similarities of thought and style between the

Tinellaria and the *Lazarillo* if studied further could tempt one to propose the name of Bartolomé de Torres Naharro to the roster of names already suggested for authorship of *Lazarillo de Tormes* (p. 22–23). One might insist that the connections are meager, and indeed they are, but in spite of this there are interesting coincidences of style and thought, if nothing more.

11. The statue had been recently unearthed and placed by the church of St. Lorenzo in Damaso. It is now at the Braschi Palace (III, 506, n. 501).

12. *Monja* ("nun") was a slang term for prostitute, and *abadesa* ("abbess") for "madam" (III, 470, n. 255).

13. The dishonesty around the cardinal's scullery and in the servants' dining room is manifested early. In the first act we learn that the servants made a big haul of food and silverware from a recent banquet (II, 205, 336–54). The quality of food served them is bad, as is brought out in the final ironic phase of act 1: "Qu'estos bocados/ no son, par Dios, de perder" ("These mouthfulls, are not to be lost, by God") (II, 209). In reality, little or nothing will be lost to the servants if they turn down the invitation to come to eat at that moment. The *bocados*, or mouthfulls, are usually not to their taste, and besides, the servants have been conditioned to depend more on their stealing from the pantry to satisfy their hunger than on the official table fare served to them.

14. In Rojas' *La Celestina*, Pármeno, a *pícaro* in his own right, derives from a similar mother. Lucrecia's characteristics surface again in the person of the washerwoman of *La lozana andaluza* by Francisco Delicado (1528).

15. The Mastro is the majordomo. Escalco (Italian, *scalco;* Spanish *mastersala*) is the one who places the food on the table and cuts the meat. He is superior to the *credenciero* ("wine keeper") and to the cook. The *despensero* ("dispenser") is not in Escalco's domain of authority (III, 469, n. 225).

Chapter Nine

1. It appears that the Marqués lives in other quarters and has no ready access to his sister's abode. When he eventually wants to enter her house he either has to call at the door (III, 561, n.265), or break the door down. If he lives there, he is apparently locked out for the night when he goes off on his own escapades.

2. Gillet and Green indicate that this second act begins on the next night following the night of the first act (*Prop.*, IV, 517). Since the opening of the door to the lover comes on a different night from that in which the promise to do so is made, the entire play would have to cover an additional night, that is, three nights, exceeding the twenty-four-hour unity of time. There is clearly some difficulty with respect to the time element of the second act. The scene remains the same as in the first act, but does it take place later on the same night, or does it take place the second night? It could be that Ymeneo and his servants return, after briefly withdrawing at the coming of Marqués and Turpedio, once the latter two were satisfied that

all was well at Phebea's house and left. Thus the courtier, Ymeneo, and his servants decide to pursue the rendezvous and serenade the maiden. The latter interpretation is one that would go well with Moratín's and Menéndez y Pelayo's conception of the duration of the play as being only twenty-four hours. (See M. Menéndez y Pelayo, *Estudios*, p. 157.)

If, as Professors Gillet and Green maintain, the play takes place in three nights, then it would embrace a significant violation of the unity of time, the prevailing norm of contemporary plays. The time element is something that, like the plot, is reminiscent of the problem of time in *La Celestina*, and is worthy of further attention. An alternative would be to view the second act as occurring later in the first night, that act 2 is merely a continuation of the first night with the approach of morning. Since the serenaders plan to return later that day, their third nocturnal appearance would make the play take place in only twenty-four hours.

3. If this action takes place still during the first night, evidently they return to the scene, probably upon hearing the singing before getting out of earshot.

4. Despite precautions, their deliberations at the door have alerted the lovers. Ymeneo has a chance to flee, whether by a back door, an upstairs or downstairs window, or even through the door as it flies open. The manner of Ymeneo's escape is not clear. Act 5 begins *in medias res* ("in the midst of things") with the confrontation between Marqués and his sister, in the presence of Turpedio and Doresta. It would appear that the confrontation takes place inside the house in Phebea's chamber, perhaps by an open window, which Phebea may have been closing when Marqués asks her, "¿Dónde vais?" ("Where are you going?") (II, 311, 2). Green begins the summary of the last act with, "The door opens and Phebea steps out into the deserted street, lighted by the dawn (Ymeneo having escaped)" (IV, 518). The arrangement of this scene is variable, for as Shergold properly indicates, we have no information about the staging of the play (Shergold, *History of the Spanish Stage*, p. 146).

If we are to suppose that there was no change of scene for the entire play, then we can imagine the stage to be divided with the street scene on one side of it, and a cutaway view of Phebea's house on the other side of the stage. There are many ways to play this scene satisfactorily, depending on the director's preferences. In the reading of the play, of course, the scene and actions are limited only by the reader's own imagination. How the escape is acted out may be puzzling, but the fact remains that the story calls for it to be carried out, and the scene therefore must be adapted to the needs of the moment.

5. Edilberto Marbán sees a similar invocation in Encina's *Égloga de Fileno y Cardonio*, which was also a part of the pastoral poetic tradition of the day. See E. Marbán, *El teatro español medieval y del Renacimiento* (New York: Las Americas, 1971), p. 149.

6. Gillet supposes that there is evidence to set the scene either in Rome or in Naples, but efforts to localize it further have thus far been unsuccessful (*Prop.*, III, 557, n. 134; 561, n. 272).

7. Beaumelle's translation is included in *Chefs d'oeuvres des théâties étrangers*, vol. 20 (Paris, 1829). The English translation can be found in *The Drama*, vol. 6 (London, 1903). See M. Menéndez y Pelayo, *Estudios*, p. 165.

8. J. Lihani, ed. Lucas Fernández, *Farsas y églogas* (New York: Las Americas, 1969); "Comedy" of Bras Gil and Beringuella (pp. 59–74), "Farce" of the Damsel (pp. 81–97), and the "Farce" of the Soldier (pp. 97–120), among others.

9. Lihani, *Lucas Fernández*, pp. 136, 149.

10. M. Romera–Navarro, "Estudio de la *Comedia Himenea* de Torres Naharro," *Romanic Review* 12 (1921), 50–73.

11. See Richard Tyler's, "False Accusation of Women in the Plays of Tirso de Molina," *Kentucky Romance Quarterly* 16 (1969), 119–23; "Algunos aspectos técnicos de la acusación falsa en Lope de Vega," in *Homenaje a William L. Fichter*, ed. A. D. Kossoff and J. Amor y Vásquez (Madrid: Castalia, 1971), pp. 725–33.

12. *Prop.*, IV, 519; Green, *Spain and the Western Tradition*, I, 120; and Crawford, *Spanish Drama before Lope de Vega*, p. 91.

13. Green, *Spain and the Western Tradition*, I, 120; M. Menéndez y Pelayo, *Estudios*, p. 157.

14. *Prop.*, IV, 518–19; and S. Gilman, "El tiempo y el género literario en *La Celestina*," *Revista de Filología Hispánica* 7 (1945), 147–59.

15. Green, *Spain and the Western Tradition*, I, 120.

16. Translation from ibid., I, 121.

17. Bartolomé de Torres Naharro, *Comedias Soldadesca, Tinelaria, Himenea,* ed. D. W. McPheeters, (Madrid: Castalia, 1973), pp. 28–29.

18. T. W. Baldwin, *On the Literary Genetics of Shakespeare's Plays* (Urbana: University of Illinois Press, 1959), pp. 521–34.

19. María Rosa Lida de Malkiel, *La originalidad artística de* La Celestina (Buenos Aires: Editorial Universitaria, 1962), p. 481.

20. I do not find him ingenuous as does McPheeters, *Comedias Soldadesca, Tinelaria, Himenea,* (p. 30). On the contrary he is bright, aggressive, confident; a long jump even from Lenicio of the *Comedia Seraphina* who also served as adviser to his master Floristán.

21. Here I agree with McPheeters, *Comedias Soldadesca, Tinelaria, Himenea,* (p. 29) that the yielding of Phebea is entirely too sudden. This same observation is made by critics about the submission of Melibea in *La Celestina*.

22. Sudden changes of mind come over other characters in Torres Naharro's work, like Liaño of the *Soldadesca*. Abrupt changes of mind come over Melibea in *La Celestina*; over Beringuella in the first "Comedy," over

Antona of the "Farce" of the Soldier, and over the Pastor of the "Farce" of the Damsel, all found in Lucas Fernández's work; over Cristino in *Égloga* XI, and over Escudero of *Égloga* VII ("Requesta de amores") of Encina. Such quick changes continue as a tradition in the Spanish theater to the seventeenth century, and persist sporadically thereafter.

Chapter Ten

1. Juan de Valdés, *Diálogo de la lengua* (Madrid: Clás. cast., 1953), p. 165.

2. J. P. W. Crawford notes the similarity of plot between the *Calamita* and other Latin plays in "A Note on the *Comedia Calamita* of Torres Naharro," *Modern Language Notes* 36 (1921), 15–17. Not only was Torres Naharro familiar with Plautus' *Asinaria* and other Latin plays, but he was likewise familiar with some of Aristotle's works. In the *Calamita,* act 4, there is a reference to *el philósopho nuestro* ("our philosopher") which is a reference by antonomasia to Aristotle (*Prop.*, III, 680).

Despite current belief to the contrary, there is evidence that Aristotle was known and studied during the Middle Ages. St. Thomas Aquinas (1226–1274) knew Aristotle, and so did others, as is shown by his *Commentaria in VIII libros Politicorum Aristotelis* (Venice, 1500), as listed by I. Kotvan in his *Inkunábuly U. Knižnice v Bratislave* (Bratislava, 1960). Scaliger may be best remembered for his work on Aristotle in the sixteenth century, but he was only one of a series of students of Aristotle that go back through the ages.

3. "From the Italian scene, at Rome where a Chigi nobleman was his patron or at Naples where he worked for Fabrizio Colonna, Torres Naharro acquired a sure knowledge of stage technique. Besides observing customs, he used novelistic devices in his plays. A scene in the fifth *jornada* of his *Calamita* is drawn from act 2, scene 9, of the *Calandria*, in which Calandro learns how to die. Torres Naharro was ready to borrow from Italians' comic themes without becoming a slavish imitator" (D. Radcliff Umstead, *The Birth of Modern Comedy in Renaissance Italy* [Chicago: University of Chicago Press, 1969], p. 237).

4. The composition of this term is based on that of "narreme." For a discussion and theory of the "narreme" see Eugene Dorfman, *The Narreme in the Medieval Romance Epic* (Toronto: University of Toronto Press, 1969). This section on recapitulation derives in part from Edward M. Malinak's "The Dramaturgy of Bartolomé de Torres Naharro" (Ph.D. diss., University of Kentucky, 1977).

5. M. Menéndez y Pelayo, *Estudios de crítica literaria*, p. 167.

6. *Century Cyclopedia of Names*, ed., B. A. Smith (New York: Century, 1894).

7. Miguel de Cervantes, *El ingenioso hidalgo Don Quijote de la Mancha*, ed., F. Rodríguez Marín (Madrid: Clás. cast., 1943), chap. 16.

Chapter Eleven

1. *Prop.*, I, 128, plate iv.
2. *Prop.*, I, 86, and plate xli.
3. R. L. Grismer, *The Influence of Plautus in Spain before Lope de Vega* (New York: Hispanic Institute, 1944), p. 143.
4. This is according to Gillet's version, while H. López Morales finds 3130 lines for the play. Approximately this length becomes a standard for the popular Golden Age plays of Lope, Tirso, and Calderón.
5. Juan de Valdés, *Diálogo de la lengua* (Madrid: Espasa Calpe, 1953), p. 164–65; Menéndez y Pelayo, *Estudios,* p. 168. In line with Valdés' thinking, the servants are more real, more human than are the masters they serve.
6. Grismer, *The Influence of Platus,* p. 146, also notes that "The *Comedia Aquilana* changes its scene of action from a garden, the trysting place of the lovers, to the rooms of the king's palace," a variation of the street scene of the Plautine comedy.
7. This is seen in the *Calamita, Ymenea, Aquilana,* and the *Seraphina.*
8. Grismer, *The Influence of Plautus,* p. 147.
9. In the *Calamita* the device of anagnorisis is taken more directly from the Latin comedy: Policiano, long-lost brother of Floristán appears after three years' absence and saves the comedy from turning into a tragedy.
10. Grismer, *The Influence of Plautus,* pp. 154–55.
11. Edited by Cejador, I, 195.
12. McPheeters, *Comedias Soldadesca, Tinelaria, Himenea,* p. 33.
13. Fernández, *Farsas y églogas,* ed. Lihani, p. 193, line 361.
14. McPheeters, *Comedias Soldadesca, Tinelaria, Himenea,* p. 32.
15. A translation of the story as "The Parable of the Whole Friend" can be found in J. E. Keller and J. R. Jones, *The Scholar's Guide* (Toronto: Pontifical Institute of Mediaeval Studies, 1969), pp. 38–41.
16. Crawford, *Spanish Drama before Lope de Vega,* p. 95.
17. See, Plutarch's *Lives,* ed. A. H. Clough, (Boston, 1906), V, 135–37. The episode of the parading beauties was also referred to by Lope de Vega in *El castigo sin venganza* (act 2, scene 16), in which Lope mentions the classical name of Antiochus itself, thus showing that he knew the story through Plutarch's version. A detailed discussion of the sources of Torres Naharro's treatment of the malingering prince can be seen in J. Lihani, "Probable Sources for Two Scenes in the *Comedia Aquilana,*" *Ariel* 1 (November, 1972), 41–47.
18. See, Thompson and Baly's *Oral Tales of India* (Bloomington: Indiana University Press, 1958), p. 218, entry H175.3. The tale is further recorded by D. N. Neogi in his *Tales Sacred and Secular* (Calcutta, 1912). There may have been additional oral versions of this story that were available for Torres Naharro but which are now unknown to us.

170   BARTOLOMÉ DE TORRES NAHARRO

19. See Crawford, *Spanish Drama before Lope de Vega*, p. 95. The date of the *Comedia del viudo* is uncertain (1514?, 1521?), although C. Stern, among others, argues for 1521. See her review of A. Zamora Vicente's edition, *Comedia del viudo* (Lisbon: Centro de Estudios Filológicos, 1962), in *Hispanic Review* 31 (1963), 359–62. If the 1514 date is preferred, then, of course, the parallels with the *Aquilana* would be due to a reversal of influence—from Gil Vicente to Torres Naharro.

20. Encina's *Égloga de Plácida y Vitoriano* (1513) performed in Italy presents a similar plaint, which may have been recalled by Torres Naharro.

21. "Apologético de las comedias españolas por Ricardo de Turia," text of A. Morel–Fatio, *Revue Hispanique*, IV, 47. Cristóbal Suárez de Figueroa also mentions *gracioso* en *El pasajero* in 1617.

Chapter Twelve

1. McPheeters, *Comedias Soldadesca, Tinelaria, Himenea*, p. 27.

Selected Bibliography

PRIMARY SOURCES

1. Editions and Texts

Propaladia. Vol. 1, edited by Manuel Cañete (Madrid: Librería de los bibliófilos, 1880); vol. 2, edited by M. Menéndez y Pelayo (Madrid: Lib. de los bibl., 1890). Volume 1 presents the plays, and volume 2 contains a useful critical study. Volume 2 has been reprinted as *Bartolomé de Torres Naharro y su "Propaladia"* (Madrid: Imp. de Fe, 1900); in *Estudios de crítica literaria* (Madrid: Hijos de Tello, 1920), pp. 9–183; and in *Edición nacional de las obras completas de Menéndez Pelayo*, vol. 7, edited by Miguel Artigas (Madrid: Consejo Superior de Investigaciones científicas, 1941), with the second title page: *Estudios y discursos de crítica histórica y literaria*, Part 2, edited by Enrique Sánchez Reyes (Santander: Aldus, 1941), pp. 269–377.

Propalladia (Madrid: Real Academia Española, 1936). A facsimile edition of the princeps of Naples of 1517 which has the material of later editions except the *Comedia Calamita* and the *Aquilana*.

"Propalladia" and Other Works of Bartolomé de Torres Naharro. Vols. 1–3, edited by Joseph E. Gillet (Bryn Mawr: University of Pennsylvania Press, 1943–51); vol. 4, *Torres Naharro and the Drama of the Renaissance*, transcribed, edited, and completed by Otis H. Green (Philadelphia: University of Pennsylvania Press, 1961). These are the most thorough studies on the complete works of the dramatist. Volume 1 contains a description of all preceding editions, and presents Torres Naharro's poetry, together with the *Diálogo del nascimiento* and its *Addición*. Volume 2 contains the critical edition of the eight remaining plays. Volume 3 has voluminous notes to the first two volumes, and volume 4 presents a synthesis of information pertinent to the author, his works and his times. Volumes 3 and 4 also offer excellent bibliographies.

Teatro selecto: Comedia Soldadesca, Ymenea, Jacinta, Calamita, Aquilana. Edited by Humberto López Morales (Madrid: Escelicer, 1970). This is an amplified version of the editor's earlier, *Tres comedias. Soldadesca,*

Ymenea y Aquilana (New York: Las Americas, 1965). It has a critical introductory commentary with a bibliography of sixteenth-century editions and modern selected critical works.

Comedias Soldadesca, Tinelaria, Himenea. Edited by D. W. McPheeters (Madrid: Castalia, 1973). Offers an informative introduction, a selected bibliography and a glossary of unusual terms.

2. Sixteenth-Century Editions

Propalladia (Naples: Joan Pasqueto de Sallo, 1524). Contents are the same as those of 1517 edition plus the *Aquilana.* A copy is located in the Library of the Hispanic Society, New York.

For a detailed description and information about the existence and location of rare sixteenth-century editions of Torres Naharro's *Propalladia,* the reader may consult the material in volume 1 of J. E. Gillet's edition of the *"Propalladia" and Other Works of Bartolomé de Torres Naharro,* pp. 5–128, and its following 58 plates. This also includes the information of A. Rodriguez-Moñino's article, "El teatro de Torres Naharro (1517–1936): Indicaciones bibliográficas," *Revista de Filología Española* 24 (1937), 37–82. Further efforts to update the information on rare copies are to be found in pertinent notes of D. W. McPheeters' edition of Bartolomé de Torres Naharro, *Comedias Soldadesca, Tinelaria, Himenea,* pp. 39–40; and in H. López Morales' edition of Bartolomé de Torres Naharro, *Teatro selecto,* pp. 9–23.

SECONDARY SOURCES

1. Books and Articles

BERTHELOT, A. "La *Propaladia* du Mans," *Bulletin Hispanique* 56 (1954), 167–74. Speaks of the Antwerp edition of the *Propaladia* which was discovered in the Municipal Library of Mans.

FALCONIERI, JOHN V. "La situación de Torres Naharro en la historia literaria." *Hispanófila* 1 (1957), 32–40. Calls Torres Naharro a perfect artist of the Renaissance, one who uses techniques of the Italian dramatists.

GILLET, J. E. "The Date of Torres Naharro's Death." *Hispanic Review* 4 (1936), 41–46. Discusses the controversy on the date of Torres Naharro's death and tentatively concludes that it falls in 1524.

GILMAN, STEPHEN. "Retratos de conversos en la *Comedia Jacinta* de Torres Naharro." *Nueva Revista de Filología Hispánica* 17 (1963–1964), 20–39. Explores the theme of Spanish Jewish converts in Rome and designates Torres Naharro as one of them.

GRISMER, R. L. *The Influence of Plautus in Spain before Lope de Vega.* New York: Hispanic Institute, 1944. Excellent discussion of the influence of this Roman dramatist on Torres Naharro's *Aquilana, Tinellaria, Seraphina, Ymenea, Soldadesca,* and *Jacinta* (pp. 142–65).

LIDA DE MALKIEL, MARÍA ROSA. "El fanfarrón en el teatro del Renacimiento." *Romance Philology* 11 (1957), 268–91. Reprinted in *Estudios de literatura española y comparada* (Buenos Aires, 1966), pp. 173–202. The Spanish soldier in *Soldadesca* is seen as an objective representation of reality and avoidance of the braggart type.

LIHANI, JOHN. "New Biographical Ideas on Bartolomé de Torres Naharro." *Hispania* 54 (1971), 828–35. Deduces that if Torres Naharro is a convert, he probably derives from Islam rather than Judaism.

LÓPEZ PRUDENCIO, J. "Los Naharro de la Torre de Miguel Sesmero." *Revista del Centro de Estudios Extremeños* 8 (1934), 161–67. Archives confirm that a Naharro family lived in Torre de Miguel Sesmero.

MCGRADY, DONALD. "*Buena ropa* in Torres Naharro, Lope de Vega and Mateo Alemán." *Romance Philology* 21 (1967), 183–85. The term derives from Italian *buona roba* ("good bedmate").

MAZZEI, P. *Contributo allo studio delle fonti, specialmente italiane del teatro di Juan del Enzina e Torres Naharro.* Lucca: Tipografia Amedei, 1922. A very good analysis of the strong influence the Italian theater had on Torres Naharro.

MEREDITH, JOSEPH A. *Introito and Loa in the Spanish Drama of the Sixteenth Century.* Philadelphia: University of Pennsylvania Press, 1928. Includes an excellent study of Torres Naharro's introits.

PICKERING, T. "A Note on the *Comedia Serafina* and *El Conde Alarcos.*" *Modern Language Notes* 71 (1956), 109–14. Dates the *Seraphina* at 1515–1517 from the use of the published version of the ballad.

RÉVAH, I. S. "Un tema de Torres Naharro y de Gil Vicente." *Nueva Revista de Filología Hispánica* 7 (1953), 417–25. Compares the presentation of the theme of the Annunciation in the *Diálogo del nascimiento* and the *Auto de Mofina Mendes* of Gil Vicente.

STERN, CHARLOTTE. "The Early Spanish Drama: from Medieval Ritual to Renaissance Art." *Renaissance Drama,* n.s. 6 (1974), 177–201. The author notes the vigorous Spanish experimentation with the dramatic mode during the period from 1490 to 1530, the excellence of Torres Naharro's *Ymenea,* and the particularity of the *Trophea.*

ZIMIC, STANISLAV. "El pensamiento humanístico y satírico de Torres Naharro." *Boletín de la Biblioteca Menéndez y Pelayo* 52 (1976), 21–100. Surveys the dramatist's ideas and finds valid points on which to differ with Gillet's interpretations.

2. Dissertations

MALINAK, EDWARD M. "The Dramaturgy of Bartolomé de Torres Naharro." Ph.D. dissertation, University of Kentucky, 1977. Discusses the art of the dramatist as exemplified in the *Comedia Ymenea, Calamita,* and *Aquilana.*

SURTZ, RONALD E. "The Birth of a Theater. Dramatic Convention in the

Spanish Theater from Juan del Encina to Lope de Vega." Ph. D. dissertation, Harvard University, 1975. First significant advance from J. P.
W. Crawford's monograph on the theater before Lope de Vega.

WEINERTH, NORA. "The Experimental Theatre of Bartolomé de Torres
Naharro." Ph. D. dissertation, Harvard University, 1976. Deals with
the creation of a new theater and the world that made it possible.
Considers the *Diálogo del nascimiento, Comedia Soldadesca, Tinellaria, Trophea,* and *Jacinta.*

Index

abbess, 91
abbot, 38, 131
accusation, —technique, 72, 99; counter—, 73; false—, 111
act, five-act division 115; transition between acts, 82
actor, 41, 19, 66, 118; —company, 38, 49, 133; Italian—, 18
Adam, 110
Africa, 67, 88
Alarcón, Hernando de, 25
Alarcos, Romance del conde, 46
Alba, Duke of, 16
alchemist, 39
Alexander, Pope, (Rodrigo Borgia), 54
Algiers, 18
Amadis of Gaul, 50
ambiguity, 80, 118
Amor y Vásquez, J., 167
anagnorisis, 125, 127, 142, 150
Andalusia, 17, 23, 33, 91, 103
antagonist, 115, 117
anticlerical sentiment, 61, 87, 100, 134
anti-Semitism, 98
aphorism, 97, 110, 119, 140
Aquila, Serafino Aquilano de' Ciminelli dall', 45, 72
Aretino, Pietro, 19
Ariosto, Lodovico, 19, 84, 110, 127, 130, 133
Aristotle, 168n2
asides, 149
audience, 28, 30–31, 33, 38, 41, 43–44, 48–49, 51, 53–54, 56–57, 73–76, 79, 82, 90, 94–96, 99, 100, 104, 110, 113–114 116–118, 122, 125–31, 135,
139, 146–47, 149, 152–54; —awareness, 48–49, nobility of, 95
authority, 131
auto, (sacramental one-act play), 32
Ávalos, Costanza d', 71; Fernando Francisco de, 18, 20, 25, 80, 84, 160n2
Ávila, Diego de, 20

Baldwin, T. W., 167n18
ballad, 29, 107
Baly, Jonas, 144, 169n18
baptism, 68, 93
Barberius, 20
baroque, 49, 108, 111, 114, 118, 121, 133, 153
Bartolo, 158n4
Bartolomé the Spaniard, 84
Basque, 93
Basurto, Rodrigo, 16, 83
Bates, A., 109
Beaumelle, Angliviel La, 109, 167n7
Belvedere Palace, 25
Bembo, Pietro, 84
Bibbiena, Cardinal, *Calandria*, 127
Bible, 45, 62, 71, 85, 113
bisoño, 55, 57
boasting, 45, 55, 57, 126; rustic, 38, 63; servant, 143; shepherd, 32
Boccaccio, Giovanni, *Decameron*, 127, 143
Borgia, Cesare, (Duke of Valentino), 18, 45, 54, 58; Rodrigo, (Pope Alexander), 54
breve comedieta, (playlet), 76
broken foot, *see pie quebrado*
brotherhood, 142

175